FOLLOWING THE FALLEN

SERVING LEADERS WHO HAVE FALLEN INTO SIN | WHAT CAN WE LEARN | & HOW DOES RESTORATION HAPPEN?

DAVE YAUK

Copyright © 2019 by The Garden City Project

www.gardencityproject.com

All rights reserved. No part of this book may be reproduced in any form or by any electronic or mechanical means, including information storage and retrieval systems, without written permission from the author, except for the use of brief quotations in a book review.

Produced in the United States of America

Ebook ISBN: 978-0-9994673-4-3

Print ISBN: 978-0-9994673-5-0

CONTENTS

1. Preface — 1

PART 1
CONTROL THE CRADLE

1. The Case Study — 13
2. The Story — 19
3. The Sin — 25
4. The Psychology (Personal Pain & Motive) — 29
5. Community Pain & Motive — 33
6. The Remedy — 37
7. Questions for Discussion — 45

PART 2
CONTRACT OF PERSONALITY VS. COVENANT OF COMMUNITY

8. The Case Study — 51
9. The Story — 55
10. The Sin — 61
11. The Psychology (Personal Pain & Motive) — 67
12. Community Pain & Motive — 71
13. The Remedy — 73
14. Questions for Discussion — 79

PART 3
CHIEFS & INDIANS

15. The Case Study — 85
16. The Story — 91
17. The Sin — 95
18. The Psychology (Personal Pain & Motive) — 99
19. Community Pain & Motive — 103
20. The Remedy — 107
21. Questions for Discussion — 119

PART 4
GIVE UP OR GIVE OUT

22. The Case Study   125
23. The Story   129
24. The Psychology (Personal Pain & Motive)   133
25. Community Pain & Motive   139
26. The Remedy   141
27. Questions for Discussion   145

PART 5
JUST A LITTLE BIT TO THE LEFT

28. The Case Study   149
29. The Story   153
30. The Psychology (Personal Pain & Motive)   159
31. Community Pain & Motive   165
32. The Remedy   171
33. Questions for Discussion   175

PART 6
BELLS & WHISTLES

34. The Case Study   179
35. The Story   183
36. The Psychology (Personal Pain & Motive)   187
37. Community Pain & Motive   191
38. The Remedy   197
39. Questions for Discussion   205

PART 7
I'LL BLOW YOUR HOUSE DOWN

40. The Case Study   209
41. The Story   213
42. The Psychology (Personal Pain & Motive)   217
43. Community Pain & Motive   223
44. The Remedy   227
45. Questions for Discussion   235

PART 8
MANIPULATIVE MAYHEM

46. The Case Study   239

47. The Story	245
48. The Psychology (Personal Pain & Motive)	249
49. Community Pain & Motive	253
50. The Remedy	257
51. Questions for Discussion	261

PART 9
MAN BEHIND THE MASK

52. The Case Study	265
53. The Story	271
54. The Psychology (Personal Pain & Motive)	279
55. Community Pain & Motive	285
56. The Remedy	291
57. Questions for Discussion	301
2. Closing Thoughts	303

1 / PREFACE

I'm broken. Imperfect. You're broken. Flawed.
Let's walk together.
Let's be healed together by our gracious Savior.

This book is all about the ways we've let ourselves down. It's all about the way our leaders have failed us. It's all about the ways in which we perceive that God has missed our expectations. Most importantly, it's all about the ways in which we've failed our God.

But wait …

This book is also about healing, restoration, redemption, and the process of mutual submission within God's family that can usher all of us into greater strength, character, and Christlikeness.

BEFORE WE DELVE into the hopeful treasures to be discovered in this work, it's important to first stop to sober ourselves in the reality of our despair without God. The reason we must ponder our own fallen condition before reading any further is that if we're not careful, we'll end up using this book as a sword of judgment to wield against all those in our life that have hurt or wronged us. You may have already felt the temptation to see a title like *Following the Fallen: Serving Leaders Who Have Fallen Into Sin; What We Can Learn and How Does Restoration Happen* only to first "think of someone else in your life that needs it." Not so fast. A better approach is to first embrace and admit one's own lie-ridden, lust-infested, idol-shaping, disappointment-natured self, in order that this book may work in us a redemptive shape of **humility**.

Humility begins to take root in us when we admit that the human condition puts us all on a level playing field. Humility begins with bad news about our condition. Ephesians 2:1-3 records it better than I can:

> And you were dead in the trespasses and sins in which you once walked, following the course of this world, following the prince of the power of the air, the spirit that is now at work in the sons of disobedience—among whom we all once lived in the passions of our flesh, carrying out the desires of the body and the mind, and were by nature children of wrath, like the rest of mankind.

Ephesians 2:1-3 is helpful to us because it cuts through the lies and tells us the truth. It tattoos all our foreheads with the same label. Equality. All are broken. It acknowledges what everyone perceives to be true, and yet won't care to admit. We all see that our world is broken, awful, hurtful, and murderous toward all who live on planet earth, and yet we can't admit that this is true of us. All the while the majority of us live and act out our hurts in fear, anxiety, and worry, causing one to ask, "Would we really act this way if we were such good people?" The above words remind us that there are no victims when it comes to sin. When left to ourselves, we all choose sin over people and God. When left without God, we are children filled with wrath—seeking only our own wants and pleasures. We will devour people, feelings, substances, technology, and any other resource on earth if it means that we can feed our flesh and what makes us most comfortable.

The Bible's portrayal of the flesh is quite different than the world's portrayal of human nature. We live in a world that goes around sporting the bumper sticker, "We're good people, and deserving of only good things." This is humanism and simply untrue. Our need to parent people into the sentimental belief that we're "good" is false. The truth is that we didn't come into this world naked and pure. We may have entered earth in our birthday suits, but we were born into a sin-entrenched world, and we came down the birth canal ingested and screaming with greed, manipulation, and hatred toward God and our fellow man.

To illustrate our childlike depravity, one of my Pastors tells the story of when one of his children was asked to leave from kids' church for biting another kid. My Pastor playfully joked that he had never once bitten his wife. His child had not learned that behavior from his parents, but had inwardly known how to outlet sin in an effort to hurt another. The proclivity to bite someone was hard-wired into the child via the DNA found also in his imperfect parents.

Sadly, we don't grow out of sin, we get better at it. More sly. More deceptive. The cycle of brokenness only grows as kids become adults. Our heads only seem to get bigger and we continue to dream up better technologies that enable us to bite each other. With our "evolved" brains, we keep dreaming up more efficient ways to gossip and slander, covet, steal and lie to each other, and the list goes on. Some call it evolution, I call it devolution.

The gospel is revolutionary, however. God is different. He's brutally honest not only about our despair but also about the hope that can be found in him. This is what I love about God. He tells us exactly what will come of us should we indulge our sinful nature and he tells us the beauty that is to be had should we run wholeheartedly toward his kingdom. There's never any secrecy with God. There's only, at best, mystery. Secrecy kills, whereas mystery invites us into the formation of a beautiful imagination. It invites conversation. It invites meditation and our growth as we imagine and press into a deeper reality beyond ourselves.

The bleak picture of Ephesians 2:1-3 is followed by the glorious news of Ephesians 2:4-10. God is equally honest about all that is good. Notice how the bad news is changed to good news in just two words, "But God":

> **But God**, being rich in mercy, because of the great love with which he loved us, even when we were dead in our trespasses, made us alive together with Christ—by grace you have been saved— and raised us up with him and seated us with him in the heavenly places in Christ Jesus, so that in the coming ages he might show the immeasurable riches of his grace in kindness toward us in Christ Jesus. For by grace you have been saved through faith. And this is not your own doing; it is the gift of God, not a result of works, so that no one may boast. For we are his workmanship, created in Christ Jesus for good works, which God prepared beforehand, that we should walk in them.

Had not God volunteered to befriend our fallen and broken humanity in the person of Jesus Christ, we would still be living in the reality of Ephesians 2:1-3. Joyously, however all humankind has new hope: the offer of grace. The kingdom of God is about grace, faith, and equality of a far different kind. As believers, we have equal access to the Father (Eph. 2:18). The Trinity invites every sinner to come and become a saint. Our Father sees that we are all broken beyond repair and he offers us all the same opportunity, to be made new (2 Cor. 5:17). The call of restoration is the call made in the gospel toward every person on earth, regardless of race or creed. A new nature is not only a hope for those dead in sin but also a sustaining promise for all those saved.

Level Ground and This Book

My plea in this preface is that we would not make the mistake of failing to find ourselves amidst the biblical stories and case studies of brokenness to be shared, or relate to them only while pointing fingers at someone else and their problems. If we only wag our finger, this book will only serve to **puff us up in pride**. It is just too easy to claim that the tragedies in the world and in the Bible have nothing to do with us. It's easier to distance ourselves, but it's not helpful. We need to embrace our own true humanity and develop an attitude of humility. We carry within ourselves the potential to bring about every atrocity witnessed in human history. Sobering, is it not?

To truly do what this book says, **to follow those who are fallen**, we can't just admit that those we have followed have hurt us; though this is true. We are also going to have to admit that at some point in life, someone is or has been following us as we've let them down. We need to lump ourselves into the bad leadership pile along with all the other bad leaders that we've known. If we're truly going to come together in communities that are healthy and led well, we are going to have to make our **imperfection** our first assumption.

Our world is plagued with fallen leaders. Our churches and corporations are riddled with immoral and broken pastors and stuffed shirts. Our methods are driven by power and result in collapse, and our communities are filled with hurt people desperately seeking any real form of transformation. God desires to bring together our shattered pieces in an effort to put back together a masterpiece-puzzle portraying love and peace.

Over my twenty years in serving the local church I've seen a need for such a masterpiece to come together. I've seen a great need within the church in particular for transformation. I've had the privilege of serving under ten different leaders that all fell tragically into public sin of some kind. Many of my most significant seasons of great brokenness came at the hands of those I was supposed to "trust." I have been an eye witness to the hell that follows fallen and broken leaders. I've observed how the wounds of others, particularly the cuts caused by the actions done by those in leadership, divided and exploded whole communities. I will venture that many of you are in the same boat.

My initial reaction to such explosions was often NOT to seek peace. My response was to scoff, run, stop trusting people, and to embrace bitterness. I now realize that sin breeds more sin. My devilish reaction to the hurts caused to me was as sinful and as harmful an action as the initial violations committed.

Many of you may have also tried to out-match the sins of others with an even more grotesque sin of your own. We've all done it. We've gossiped. We've maligned. We've sarcastically backhanded those who have hurt us with veiled comments. We've angled at revenge. We've held onto bitterness within like a poison we hoped might kill our enemy, only to wake up and realize we've killed ourselves from the inside out.

I want to exhort you. I want to tell you that after all my time spent simmering in hurt and anger, I came to understand that serving under and alongside these leaders was a privilege. Yes, a privilege. They taught me about my own humanity. In being hurt by them, I was also healed because of them. In being exposed to their pain, I was exposed. In being sinned against, I was able to learn of the sins deep within my own heart: these hurts that billowed forth in rage, strife, slander, malice, and hatred.

If you're a hurting human, let me first validate your pain. Feel comforted, heard, and at ease. We're all in this together. But please also feel my urgent plea to you to lay down your protective walls. Let them fall. Doing so will lead us to seek a greater remedy by encouraging each other toward complete healing. Complete healing is found in the ability to trust and love again.

Now that I have processed my own grief in the aftermath of these various tragedies, I find myself filled with love for the communities and churches left in heartache over the broken trust and messes left behind. I want to see whole families, churches, and communities heal. I want to see them healed together in a way like never before. I want to see the Body of Christ become the "one another" and "household" of God that Paul speaks about. True "oneness" comes through a lot of tears and is forged under the influence of a lot of thunder and waves.

So embrace the storm, and let's keep sailing toward the horizon.

Nothing New Under the Sun

As Solomon would tell us, there's "nothing new under the sun." Therefore, you are going to see this sentiment in every chapter. The outline for every chapter will be very much the same.

I will begin by sharing the real stories of real leaders and situations I've experienced in the past. I will use fake names, embellished scenarios, and slightly different circumstances in my descriptions so as to avoid casting any shadows of shame on anyone and to avoid intentionally exposing them. I will, however, tell the stories honestly. I will attempt to relive them in a way that is dignified, and in a manner to which we can all relate. You'll most likely find that these stories are to some degree your story. They've happened to you. They've happened around you. They've happened to those you love.

Next, I will dig deeper into a passage and/or story of Scripture that deals with a similar situation. Again, there is nothing new under the sun. All of what we encounter in life, good or bad, has been experienced before. God has carefully included within his story the story of humanity so that we can relate to and find a great deal of peace in reading about people that have gone through similar things as us. It's very interesting how there's nothing quite more freeing and instructive than reading about, and almost reliving in our mind's eye, the secrecy and torment of others in Scripture. In living out the stupidity of many of the Bible's characters and seeing how God extended them grace and mercy beyond compare, we can bring a little bit of that health, honesty, steadfast love, and spiritual presence into our own feelings of betrayal, abandonment, and sense of injustice.

Following my attempts to rightly tell the stories of my experience and of the Scriptures, I'll delve into the **psychology and sociological** struggles that form as a result of the sins committed. Though I will make the disclaimer up front that I'm not a psychologist, I will rely heavily on the inspiration I've drawn from respected thinkers in these areas to bring needed insight. I'll do so not out of the belief that psychology and sociology help with the remedy to our problem of sin, but more than anything, with the view that they help us diagnose the problem. Since we often get so mad at the offender when injustice strikes, we don't often take time to consider what brought them to do what they did. We don't ponder the psychological effects that led up to, occurred during, and came from their sin. In the same manner, we don't fully digest what seeds of disunity and distrust may have emerged in the soil of our own souls or in the community where the sin took place. Dissecting each leadership experience and pairing it with the stories of Scripture might just help us humanize those we've demonized. They always say it's hard to hate someone up close. Coming near to our real heart issues may help us more thoroughly process each variable, resulting in our lives being enriched with wisdom and character.

Lastly, in every chapter, we will come face-to-face with the gospel. The remedy. This may sound simple, and yet it's profound. Why? Because this book is not just a book about **boundaries** or **conflict resolution**. This is not just a self-help book of information, but rather an attempt to see transformation come into situations—making all involved better than they were before or ever could have been. ***I will provide helpful biblical solutions at the end of every chapter that I feel will help bring complete healing to broken people, leaders, and communities, no matter the time, place, or circumstance.***

I will not dumb down the gospel in seeking trite solutions. I think it's just too easy to simplify truth to the simple idea that "Jesus saves sinners" and leave it only at that. Though he does indeed save sinners, the scriptures also tell us that he "fills all in all." Jesus came to dwell with a redeemed **people** in a redeemed **way of life**. Therefore, the health of our communities, the reconciliation of tattered relationships, and the recommitment to doing things better on into the future is a more complete view of the gospel. The good news of Jesus not only transforms the past, present, and future of a community in tears, but he reawakens a groaning creation. His good news beckons harmony amongst man and beast, angel and human, and heaven and earth. The gospel restores and redeems all things. It brings us back to each other.

In looking at the gospel through a beautifully full lens, I think we'll find greater meaning in our pains, greater opportunity in our injustices, greater pleasures afforded to us beyond embracing our sins or the sins committed against us, and a greater love from the kingdom that emerges, forms, and flourishes because of all the gold uncovered underneath the soot of our shame. I pray that those offended and any offenders would receive the deepest of healings. I pray that any work done in this book won't just help us all work through what was done wrong, or what went wrong, but it will ultimately lead us to put in place better paradigms for serving each other as we grow together as a family.

Much of our power structures today, even within the family of God, result from our deep hurts and fears, not from a deep place of health. Taking a look at all our fallen hope in a holistic way will ensure greater health and faith within the people of God far into the future.

∽

> ***Father***, *help us gain insight into the depth of our wrongs. In doing so, may we learn great patience and mercy in dealing with the wrongs of others.*

> ***Jesus***, *teach us how you fill all things, redeem all things, and reconcile all things broken back to yourself so that we may be used as Spirit-filled agents; extending your forgiveness and love freely to those who have offended us.*

> ***Holy Spirit***, *comfort us with your counsel, conviction, and care. As a broken yet reconciled people, make us One, as you, the Father, and Jesus are One. Amen.*

PART 1
CONTROL THE CRADLE

1 / THE CASE STUDY

Chuck carries himself in the manner worthy of a Pastor. When he passes by people walking down the halls or out in the community, everyone manages to catch the shimmer in his smile and the twinkle in his eye. More often than not he stops to lay his hand lovingly on someone's back or extend a cordial handshake. He's like that with everyone. He's kind, he's funny, and he's charming. The kids love him, the adults love him, and the church loves him. He's a gifted speaker and teacher, and his demeanor is always warm and welcoming. Just hearing him teach brings challenge, comfort, and conviction.

Chuck loves God. Chuck's family loves God, particularly his daughter Claire. Out of all their children—and they have a massive family of seven—Claire is the brightest light. Even though she comes off a bit artsy, a tad flighty, and generally an odd duck, it's clear she hails from the bloodline of her father. Her smile lights up a room, and all her youth leaders see her as the person they trust the most. She's kind to the stranger, welcoming to every kid that sits alone in the room by themselves, and she always seems to know the right Bible verse to quote in order to get every answer correct.

Chuck and Claire ... they are perfect ... or so it seems.

Below the facade of cheery pleasantry lies a pervasive sense of control in both Chuck and Claire. One cannot express it in words, but it can be felt. For example, if you disagree or challenge either one of them, their smile turns to a short smirk. If you vouch for anything new, their jaw clinches and their posture slumps a bit, as if to yell: "we don't change."

Simon is one of the Associate Pastors at the church. Simon is a godly man who also has a large family: more than ten. The first thing anyone notices, especially those who were raised in broken homes, is Simon's commitment to his wife and kids. His love for his family is incredibly unique. Different. Carefree somehow. Honest. Filled with integrity. Real.

Simon also has a gift. He tends to be able to see through people. He uses his gift for good. As he sees into the lives and deepest sins of hundreds of teenagers and their families, he still seems to offer hope to them. He is known to be very intuitive and straightforward, but once he finds a secret, he never pounces to devour people like prey. He cares. He listens. He instructs. He walks with people through their pain. He leads them to the grace to be found in Jesus.

Simon acts the same toward Chuck and Claire. One day Chuck and Claire come in contact firsthand with the discerning gaze of Simon. With very simple and loving questions he uncovers their secrets and rebellion. As the truth begins to billow out like a volcano spewing on the floor, Chuck and Claire struggle to admit they have failures. They're "religious." And yet, if they would only listen, Simon is able to so gently and wisely apply God's Word in order to help heal their hurts.

Suffice it say, when "real" clashes with pleasantry, an explosion happens. Simon, Claire and Chuck witness the explosion. Simon gently peels away layer upon layer of Chuck's and Claire's souls. He discovers very quickly that Chuck is a very angry man.

He is verbally harsh with his wife, controlling of her position in the family, and he cares very little about the plans and aspirations of others. When confronted on these issues by Simon, he just throws back his head in nervous annoyance, walks off, and carries on doing "what he is called to do."

Chuck is like that. He hides behind "what he is called to do." It is his front for what he wants to do. He has the elders tied around his finger, and every family member of the church wrapped up in his cordial handshakes. Time after time after one encounters him, it seems there is just a hanging question mark that lingers as if to wonder: "There is just something that is not right with that guy."

The issue?? Control.

Chuck prizes his reputation. He prizes his way. He serves only at the feet of what people think of him. He controls people's perception through manipulation while only letting those closest to him know the truth. That's what closeness does—it exposes who we really are. Chuck works very hard to let no one get closer than a handshake. But Simon gets too close. Claire has already gotten too close.

Claire's closeness affords her the ability to see all of her Father's pain. He uses her as an outlet. Though Claire attempts to handle her silent struggles with her Father with equal and yet twisted control, her mask is not quite as bulletproof. She plays the fool, though she is cunning. She pretends to be righteous, and yet her crusade to help the outcasts and the rebels in the youth group are really her silent confession that she is the outcast. She's the rebel.

While Daddy is away doing ministry, Claire plays. She drinks. She flirts with guys only to heighten her sense that she can control them. The men in her family are out of her control at home, so she finds men she can snatch up at school that are drawn in by her smile.

KJ is one of those guys. KJ is 24 years old and one of the Pastors in training at the church. He's handsome. He is a star athlete. The only thing he excels in more than sports is immaturity. He's young. Yes, he's a big kid inside. Maybe fourteen? Perhaps it's the 14-year-old inside of him that takes notice of Claire.

As the closeness grows between the 24-year-old KJ, and the 14-year-old Claire, they seem to live under the delusion that no one notices their twinkling eyes, but Claire's friends see clearly that something inappropriate is beginning. One person, in particular, sees everything. With eyes wide open. Simon.

As I said, when real meets pleasantry, an explosion is just waiting to happen.

KJ and Claire progress in their relationship behind closed doors. What begins as playful back rubs, tickling each other's hands between the seats at movies, and car rides home under false pretenses, turns into a passionate and explosive love affair. Kissing. Sex. Scandal.

Simon notices that the car rides home get more frequent. He follows one night. He discovers that the car does not head toward Claire's home at all, but out into the vacant countryside. No lights. No exposure. As Claire and KJ pull over in an effort to "keep their love a secret," Simon knocks on the window. The jig is up. Secrecy is exposed. The religious front collapses.

Claire's fake smile that almost never changes, is now gone. Simon's kindness, on the other hand, is still steady. It never changes. This time is no different. He gently ushers them out of the car, escorts them into his, drives them to Chuck's house, and proceeds alongside them into and through the night to begin the discussion that has been a long time in waiting.

Chuck's reaction is not what Simon hopes for, however. The exposure of Claire exposes Chuck. Remember … Control! His perfect facade is threatened, and rather than let the walls come down in openness, honesty, and in a manner that invites healing, Chuck hardens. He stiff-arms Simon. He silences Simon. He warns him that if he tells a soul that he will take action against Simon to ruin his life.

At that moment, Simon relents. He walks away. Back to life as usual. He's a Shepherd, and a kind one at that, but not a fighter. He avoids the issue. In the weeks ahead Claire and KJ distance themselves from each other. Chuck continues handshaking, and Simon sits in the corner pretending to be free while his hands are tied. Each person attempts to avoid an explosion by living in denial. Claire pretends to let rebellion go, Simon lets authenticity die, KJ pretends to grow up, and Chuck, well, he continues on as normal.

All the people explode inside under Chuck's pressure. Except for Chuck. His showmanship is impenetrable. Bullet Proof.

Needless to say, stories like this never end well, and they always end quickly. KJ did not last more than two more weeks. His heart was never into God anyway. He was only into Claire. He left. Simon quenched his honesty for only so long, but one day felt compelled to burst into Chuck's office with the elder team to confront Chuck. The confrontation was done in kindness in an effort to lovingly restore Chuck's family and to fight for greater safety between the leadership and youth. That's not how Chuck interpreted it.

Claire only became more rebellious and bitter at Simon for ousting her. She left the youth group.

Simon unexpectedly quit his job two months later, but everyone involved knew that he had been fired. Chuck still attempted to maintain his composure, but it only lasted two more years. The people at the church began to encounter Chuck's temper. They began seeing the real man through the pleasant handshakes. They got close. Too close. Right at the time that the church was seeking to call Chuck to accountability out of a spirit of love and concern for him, Chuck left under the mask of this statement, "I feel called to Pastor a church in Arizona."

He never relinquished control!

2 / THE STORY

The Saga of Chuck, Simon, Claire, and KJ seems like an all too familiar scenario in our world today. Regrettably, what we often fail to understand in these situations is that the Bible records similar scenarios to help us wisely walk through them, understand them, and come to complete reconciliation and healing with our Lord, ourselves, and with each other. Therefore, before jumping too head-long into the situation mentioned in The Case Study, let's consider a Biblical story that carries similar destructive DNA.

THE KING of the Ammonites dies, and Hanun his son reigns in his place (2 Sam. 10:1). This is the scene in 2 Samuel 10.

King David rules and reigns over God's people as King, and in response to the king of the Ammonite's death, David sends his servant to go and console Hanun regarding the death of his father. As the servants approach Hanun's country, his princes and advisors whisper deceitful questions in the king's ear; "Do you think because David has sent comforters to you, that he is honoring your father? Has not David sent his servants to you to search the city and to spy it out and to overthrow it" (2 Sam. 10:3)?

Hanun and his leadership council misinterpret the situation; falling prey to believing that real malicious intent lies beneath the pleasantry of King David. Hanun believes David's advance to be veiled, half-hearted, and secretive. Out of competition and jealousy, they assume David to be the enemy. In doing so, they take David's servants and shame them by cutting their beards and garments in half. All efforts are made to shame King David and the people of God.

Doubting David's intentions comes at a price, however. In their betrayal, the Ammonites sense they have become a stench to David. They immediately call for reinforcements. They hire the Syrian army to come to help protect them. When David hears of this, he sends out Joab and all the host of his mighty men to meet both the Ammonite and the Syrian army.

But the Ammonites and Syrians flank Joab. The Ammonites set the battle against David's army, both in the front and in the rear. Being quick on his feet, Joab commissions half of David's army to fight against the Ammonites—led by his brother Abishai—and half of the army to fight the Syrians.

The Israelite blow is terrifying and crushing. It overtakes the Syrians; scaring them back into hiding, and it frightens the Ammonites into retreat. Nevertheless, their cowardice does not last long. Pulling back with their tails between their legs is a humiliating posture and a hard pill to swallow, particularly for the Syrian armies. Because of their shame and inability to admit defeat, we see in 2 Samuel 10:15-16 that the Syrian's regather their troops, and they come out once again to the field of battle to seek a rematch with King David's armies. This time is different. David does not send Joab or Abishai, but the text says, "when it was told David, he gathered all Israel together and crossed the Jordan and came to Helam" (vs. 17). Needless to say, it is a massacre. David overtakes 700 chariots, 40,000 horsemen, and kills Shobach, the commander of the Syrian army.

2 Samuel 10 ends with these words; "so the Syrians were afraid to save the Ammonites anymore" (vs. 19).

This story is a tragic tale of misperception and distrust between two leaders, but I've included it in order to set up what comes next. Not long after this in the springtime, 2 Samuel 11 tells that it is again time for war. It is time for David's armies not only to defeat the Syrian army, but to enact revenge on the Ammonites. However, this time, when the soldiers go out to battle, we are specifically told that David remains in Jerusalem.

The text never tells us about the motives David has in choosing not to fight with his men, but we are told that David is immediately drawn into sin in the wake of his negligent decision not to go. We are all most likely familiar with what comes next … David commits adultery with Bathsheba.

Bathsheba is the wife of one of the soldiers in David's army, Uriah. As David stays back ogling Bathsheba, naked while taking a bath on her rooftop, Uriah leaves to fight the Ammonites. David allows his battle for revenge and honor against the Ammonites to be handled by others. At this moment he doesn't play the warrior, he retreats as the coward and becomes the fool.

To make a long story short, King David commands that Bathsheba come into his household. David sends messengers this time, not to fight in the war, mind you, but to get for himself what he desires. They bring her to David, clean and prepare her for him, and David lies with her and gets her pregnant.

Preparation for a perfect explosion.

David enters a frenzy. *How's he going to cover it up*? He calls Uriah off of the battle field and orders him to go and lay with his wife. Uriah, however, a faithful soldier, sleeps at the gates that night; believing that he is undeserving of a pleasurable night with his wife while his soldiers are out dying for the cause of David's kingdom.

David's frenzy heightens. *What is he going to do*? He again calls Uriah to his quarters. This time he hands Uriah a letter that is being delivered immediately to Joab on the battlefield. Undisclosed to Uriah, the contents of the letter command Joab to put Uriah on the front lines of the fighting so that he will surely be killed. David fails in his attempt to cover up his act with Bathsheba and resorts to murder.

Bathsheba is made the wife of David, and she ends up bearing him a son—the next King. Solomon. But we must not forget that during this entire season of control, betrayal, deception, and cover-up, that lurking off in the shadows all this time is a glimmer of purity amidst a dark mess: David's friend Nathan.

Nathan's silence lasts only so long, and then, forced to speak out of conviction to right the wrong, he bursts into David's quarters and tells him a parable:

> There were two men in a certain city, the one rich and the other poor. The rich man had very many flocks and herds, but the poor man had nothing but one little ewe lamb, which he had bought. And he brought it up, and it grew up with him and with his children. It used to eat of his morsel and drink from his cup and lie in his arms, and it was like a daughter to him. Now there came a traveler to the rich man, and he was unwilling to take one of his own flock or herd to prepare for the guest who had come to him, but he took the poor man's lamb and prepared it for the man who had come to him.

David again enters into a frenzy. He is beside himself with anger at a rich man who would do such a thing to a poor man. David draws his sword in hopes to search out, find, and kill this heathen. He flails about. He shouts. He spits. And Nathan brings David to shame and says: "You are the man!"

David's world collapses. The facade of control falls. Pleasantry is made into honesty. Lies lose to the truth. His very own child dies as a result of his entire plot. The Lord is displeased with David.

Everything that can explode did.

3 / THE SIN

Most likely you are trying to create a parallel between King David's fake pleasantry, which erupted in adultery and murder, with that of Chuck's story of a fake cover-up and control. But we must not be too quick to shout out the obvious token sins like adultery, murder, lies, and statutory rape. In blurting out cardinal vice too quickly we may miss the more subtle origin of sin itself. The heart!

In the case of King David, his sin began long before his thirsty eye met Bathsheba. It began in his heart. In the scenario with the Amorites directly preceding David's fall over Bathsheba, did you catch the genesis of the "real" problem? Did you see where sin began to germinate? The whole ruse started when David set out to console a hurting son after the death of his father. Hanun misinterpreted David's compassion and real pursuit. He labeled David unjustly as a rabblerouser, a fight starter, and a spy. The accusations pierced David's heart like arrows. They hurt. They confused. They complicated. All injustice hurts, frustrates, and makes matters worse.

David carried this wound. He was fine with letting Joab scare back the Ammonites and Syrians, but he was not about to let Joab go it alone when the Syrians came out of hiding to try and fight again. David himself went out. He fought for his reputation. He began warring from a place of being wronged. He was no longer fighting for a people or for his God, but for himself. He won. Sure. He destroyed the Syrian army, and he went on to strike fear into the Ammonites and any other army who would seek to become his enemy again. It was a statement.

And yet, it was a statement that the Ammonites did not learn. They came out to fight again. Why? David's first attempt with Hanun was to make friends, but his desire turned to competition, power, and control. David stands pitted against the line of Hanun in ironic contrast. He's not a strong warrior who desires power as Hanun, but he's a coward who slinks back into his couch cushions. He takes up his binoculars in order to grab at control and power all the same—yet in other forms. Adultery.

David's mission for sex takes on the same DNA as that of his enemies. We become what we judge, after all. David's bitterness toward the Ammonites turned him into a vengeful warrior and then into a willing coward. Adultery is never the germ, merely the symptom. David, a once wee shepherd boy, had been rattled in his security as a man. All his actions in 2 Samuel stem from insecurity; a heart bent away from God, and a heart doubting all that God has already given him.

The almost hidden sin of the whole story is insecurity. It's bitterness. It's hurt. All these things led David to avoid his responsibility as a leader (2 Sam. 11:1). He gave in to idle hands and chose not to fight, which allowed him to be overtaken by evil, indulging himself during the day time (2 Sam. 11:2). What's more atrocious, he then enters into discontent and competition with the Ammonites, Uriah, and even himself. The competition turns him into a thief. His discontent turns him into an adulterer, and his desire turns him into a monster.

Through it all, Nathan points out the ridiculousness of it all.

Though David owns the cattle on a thousand hills, David loses sight of all that he has, only to take from Uriah what little was afforded to him. It's absolute nonsense. Could it be that all sin is born out of discontent, thanklessness, and bitterness? Heart issues?

The story of King David's troubles is very instructive for us in understanding Chuck's, KJ's, Claire's, and Simon's in our own lives. Chuck's life didn't start with control. His mere dishonest pleasantry existed only to protect something deeper. KJ's sin didn't start with a desire for statutory rape. It's deeper. Claire's rebellion and control of men didn't start with her Dad. It began with her embracing the lie that she had to pretend to be someone else in order to be loved.

To discover how we are to move forward when destructive sin takes hold, we need to really pastorally understand people and situations before pronouncing solutions and judgments.

4 / THE PSYCHOLOGY (PERSONAL PAIN & MOTIVE)

Psychology literally means "the study of the soul." Humans are soulish creatures. We are different in our soul (*nephesh*) than animals, in that we can express analytical thought. We possess true language and conceptual ability. We can determine, learn from, and explore our history. We are economic beings. We are aesthetic beings—in search of beauty. We have a conscience, and we desire to worship and give honor.

Where Psychology can prove most useful is in the exploration of our soul. As we explore our soul, the Bible says we're going to find nothing but broken, incomplete, and dissatisfied pieces. Therefore, Psychology should not be viewed as a problem solver, but merely as a diagnostic tool. Psychology is filled with metaphors that allude to and affirm our destructive superego, and it challenges us to change our behavior in an effort to produce a more unified healthy self, yet it never helps us toward any lasting solutions. Though it boasts great healing power, it merely forwards us to the conclusion that we are frail and unable to fix ourselves. The more we contemplate our issues, it seems the more problems we find, and Psychology can't fix the heart. Psychological contemplation can, however, really be helpful if we use it correctly. It can help us uncover the depth of our need, the depth of our humanity, our realness, and the real poverty that exists within our soul without God. When we think about Chuck, KJ, Simon, Claire, King David, and even characters like Nathan or Hanun, our goal should be to uncover what lies in the depths of people, just beyond the surface. We need to aim to cure the germ, not treat symptoms.

In many ways, adultery, control, performance, vengeance—and the list goes on—are symptoms of deeper evils that drive each and every human. If we're going to heal, we have to receive God's love at the place of our sin's origin.

King David's original hurt in the story came after the Ammonite King had died. David pledged his loyalty and affection to Hanun, the son of Nahash (the previous king), and yet when David's team arrived to provide support and consolation, David's servants were shamed, his motives were accused, and David embraced the situation personally at the deepest level. This is where David's buttons were pressed. He had nothing pushing him toward adultery, murder, deception, and evil until he suffered a situation that hurt him. It undid him. He lost all sight of who he was in God, and whose he was, and embracing lies of abandonment and insecurity birthed in him all the sins that ensued.

At the deepest level, David's sin is pride. You may respond, "No, it is insecurity." Well, yes, sort of. **Pride is really insecurity in reverse.** Like David, we all have places in us that need to find satisfaction, and rather than admitting our weakness, we act like we don't need any help. Our masquerade only continues until someone bumps into our insecurity and exposes us.

If we are secure in "whose we are" as God's kids, there's really no need to doubt ourselves regarding our worth, nor is there a reason for us to inflate ourselves and try to act bigger. David gave in to the biggest sin of all. He doubted his value, dignity, and worth as God's son.

David's personal pain was caused only by the sin of unbelief. He forgot the goodness of his God and forgot his frailty as a man, and he uttered the words, "I should be treated better than this." Statements of entitlement open up doors to every kind of rebellion and indulgence and often close the door to God's glory being realized in our situation. It's almost as if for a second David forgot about the nature of mankind—our destructive hurtful ways—and assumed Hanun would just hug him. David forgot about what pain and heartache can do to people. He forgot also what pain causes people to do, and he expected, as we all do, that only good things should come to him.

Hanun wounded David's pride. Wounded pride is where all bitterness begins. The seed plants, the roots spread, and the bitter tree starts to grow up to defile many (Heb. 12:15). We must ask ourselves if the same is the case with Chuck, Claire, KJ, and Simon. We might first assume that Chuck's cardinal sin is control. It's not. It's pride. Chuck, like King David, could not stand for his name and reputation to be tarnished. Though Chuck did not commit adultery or actually murder anyone, he went so far as to cover up his insatiable lust for self-preservation by firing Simon, and he covered up the sexual sin of his daughter and KJ by doing as King David had done—by avoiding all responsibility to do what is right.

Ultimately, the Chucks of our world are **reversely proud**. They are insecure inside, and so everyone around them sees pride outside. They protect their image, name, and reputation at all costs because they want to believe people need them; even though they know this is not true. They believe they deserve to be respected and paid high esteem. They believe their ways are the only ways, and they will do everything they can to be the Savior and Lord in every situation. Trouble is, when one tries to get close to them, too close, the mask comes off. The real person is revealed.

Chuck didn't like being exposed, nor did Claire—she left the youth group. She rejected closeness. KJ too. They all rejected closeness. And why? It's the same reason we all reject closeness at times. We're afraid someone is going to see the unlovable side of us that we see, and it will confirm what we already know is true. We're unlovable.

In all reality, closeness is the best thing for us. Being close to each other brings out what is really there. It allows people to see the true us. Brokenness and all. When we allow our brokenness to show itself freely, then we can allow others to speak into our pain and bring real truth and healing. Otherwise, without truthful community around when we do "bear all," we'll end up becoming like the bearded lady in the acclaimed movie, *The Greatest Showman.* We'll walk around like an open sore amongst others that also bear similar sores. We won't heal, we'll just feel validated. We'll believe we are O.K. to a degree, as we'll sing "we're broken and bruised" with the people around us, yet we'll neglect the needed truths necessary to bring healing. I fear there are too many Chucks, King Davids and bearded ladies in our world walking around sporting the mantra, "This is Me, deal with it" while continuing to identify themselves with their pain rather than in seeking healing.

5 / COMMUNITY PAIN & MOTIVE

The sin of those who are fallen effects the individual and it wreaks greater havoc on the community. Obviously, we could just dumb down sin's affects by using blanket statements such as; "David murdered, which took a husband and father away." Or, "David lied, which hurt his whole army. He committed adultery and because of it Bathsheba was used, abused, and left to our own guilt and shame, etc." These statements, though they are all true, are too easy.

Hear me! I'm not belittling the consequences of any of David's actions. I'm also not belittling the fact that Chuck's actions destroyed his family and credibility, or that Claire's lustful approach led KJ astray. Rather, I want to explore in these short community sections what kind of community our sins form.

When Chuck controlled everyone with his pleasant smile and pleasant handshakes, his mask taught everyone how to act. They were to be fake. Pristine. Perfect. He modeled cover up. He modeled deception, shame, and manipulation. This, in turn, led others to follow suit. Claire, Chuck's daughter and student of Chuck, learned the role of "perfect." She learned to conceal her sins. Consider also where this led Simon. In this particular story, one might even call him the hero, but even though he was a family man, a caring person, and an upright man, he was sucked into the lies of the community in concealing sin.

When the time came for Simon to stand up and confront the situation, he chose to do nothing—at least for a while. Chuck's control had created an atmosphere of fear. No one could contradict him. No one could stand up to him. No one could do anything. When they did ... Fired!

Likewise, when David decided to go on a bloody rampage of revenge against the Syrians and Ammonites, it taught his soldiers the real reason they faught. He taught them fighting is for revenge, not justice. Is that right? No. Wrong. David also put the friend he loved, Nathan, in an uncomfortable position. It is uncanny how similar Nathan is to Simon. He seems naturally an insightful encourager. A Friend. He was naturally someone who supports, not confronts, and yet Nathan was forced to wrestle with issues he shouldn't have had to wrestle with because he was scared of the King. Let's face it, Nathan was thinking; "if David would go to such great lengths as to murdering Uriah in his cover-up, what could he possibly do to me?"

When controlling leaders lead, communities adopt their leader's posture. People start to look for things they can control because the world allowed them is out of their control. What comes about as a result is all kinds of evil. Control brings on greater "controllers" such as disorders, addictions, rebellions, mental illnesses, and on and on and on.

Take for example **Communism** as we consider the communal effects of control. From the day the Bolsheviks seized power in Russia in 1917, dozens of attempts have been made across the globe to establish societies based on Communist principles. It devastates economies because people stop producing. It destroys a people's history because all that is allowed to be remembered and celebrated is the desires of the dictator. Dictators take what they want when they want.

Consider the example of the Soviet Union. One of the reasons they had such a hard time establishing a market economy after the days of communism is because no one had any respect for people's wishes, land rights, or personal boundaries. The Soviet leadership took what they wanted.

Similar to Chuck's case with Simon, dictators tend to imprison, get rid of, or silence those who might disagree. Closed control causes people to stop questioning, stop caring, stop learning, and ultimately stop defending what is right. It allows the one at the top to continue to do what's wrong, and the community begins to willingly enable the leader through passive behavior.

We know that a controlling way of life leads to slavery and the wrong treatment of people. Perhaps this is why after so many years of oppression, the Israelites still wanted to go back to Egyptian slavery. They'd forgotten how to be free. Perhaps this is why they kept walking into idol after idol, and God had to keep allowing them to go into exile after the exile.

It's easy as a people to lose our desire to be free. Like the Israelites, we simply make our peace with slavery. Throughout the Old Testament, when the Lord tried to lead his people to freedom, it's as if they resisted. They welcomed the bondage of their sin rather than embracing the promise of freedom. When the Lord would speak and lead them to what he defined as good, the people struggled to trust. It was easier for them to resort back to being controlled, and we're just as open to the same thing.

As we walk into the next section and consider how the Gospel —the remedy—addresses these elements of individual sin and community brokenness, let's ponder how all that we've mentioned to this point might influence a person's understanding of the gospel, and the intent of the Lord in the good news.

6 / THE REMEDY

So How Do We Heal? How Do We Find Freedom Again?

Controlling, vengeful, lustful, and competitive leaders cause the people under them to actually thirst for that same control. I said before that people can actually lose a sense of what freedom is like. Even today, we have some of the most venomous angry protests erupting regularly that champion some of the world's deepest bondages. People who have been sexually assaulted in any form flaunt the hurt done to their bodies, spirit, and psyche through their homosexuality; parading around in so-called "pride" while overlooking the real freedom of humility.

People willingly welcome the hurt, death, and never-ending psychological guilt and torment that results from aborting babies and call it freedom. Women's rights activists champion prostitutes and strippers as being "strong and free women," and yet balk at the abuse of women in pornography and those being raped. People under the world's system are not crying out for freedom, they are crying out for more bondage.

The beautiful gospel transforms everything. It doesn't just free us from sin, it retrains our palettes to desire true freedom again. Consider the words of Romans 7:4-6:

> Likewise, my brothers, you also have died to the law through the body of Christ, so that you may **belong to another**, to him who has been raised from the dead, in order that we may bear fruit for God. For while we were **living in the flesh**, our sinful passions, aroused by the law, were at work in our members to **bear fruit for death**. But now **we are released** from the law, having died to that which **held us captive**, so that we **serve in the new way of the Spirit** and not in the old way of the written code.

The written code is itself bondage. The way the world works is bondage. However, we have a new way to follow. One of the Spirit. And did you catch the language of control vs. freedom in the above passage? The law binds us and destines us to move toward death. Dead people do dead things, but Paul says we were "released" by the new way of the Spirit.

The way of the Spirit is one of complete freedom within healthy boundaries set for our safety. God is not a control freak. He's so secure in who he is that he can equip, empower, and release people for ministry. He's not in need of validation and he doesn't lead us with fake pleasantry to trick us into loving him. He is inwardly fortified. He's a fortress of confidence. He's bulletproof.

Thinking about God as being unshakeable and yet also thinking about him as honest—as one wrapped in a mystery and yet a certainty, an owner of all things and yet a giver, and a hater of flesh but yet a lover of real pleasure—encourages us all in our own struggle with control. God's very nature encourages us to give up our control of the belief that he has something better. It encourages all of us who have welcomed control to name it as bondage and to take the first steps into God's liberty.

In the following section to close this chapter, I'm going to suggest a few ways that the gospel can bring real healing and redemption to our places of control. It can save those that have been hurt by a Pastor's moral failure or who have done the failing themselves. It can reshape a leader's OCD and heal a community that has learned to thirst for it. The gospel redeems the people over us that have taken advantage of us in some adulterous or murderous way and allows us to forgive rather than grow bitter. The gospel also allows us to better think through paradigms and forms for leadership that better promote flourishing for all those involved.

The Gospel Teaches Us About the Safety Found in a Trinitarian Leadership Paradigm

Let's start at the beginning. The Trinity. Our God is an "us." He's three, and yet he's the *shamah*—our God is ONE. As the Old Testament unfolds, we see many glimpses of our Trinitarian God acting within the story, but none quite so clear as in the very moments when leadership fails most.

For example, in the days of Samuel, all the people came to Samuel and started complaining about the leadership style of their unseen, Triune-but-One God. They asked for a good-looking visible King to rule them. They wanted what all the other nations had: a single leader to call their own.

Though God clearly demonstrates his sadness at their request (1 Sam. 15) he relents through Samuel, and the people get their King: Saul. Nonetheless, even in light of humanity's treachery, God remained faithful. He would preserve his Triune image among humanity. In his extraordinary wisdom, he raised up Samuel who was known as a prophet, a priest, and a judge (their equivalent to a king at that time). Samuel was ONE man and yet operated in THREE offices—prophet, priest, and king. God was going to uphold his Trinitarian image on earth despite human rebellion.

Though the people wanted one Senior Leader, God continued to lead his nation via a Triune/Multiplicity leadership model of Prophets, Priests, and Kings. Each of these offices to some degree reflects how each member in the Trinity interacts and relates in community and completion. This carried all the way through into the ministry Jesus, where he united, once again, all three of those offices together in Himself as the ultimate Prophet (Mt. 17), Priest (Heb. 4:14-16), and King (Mt. 21:1-11).

The New Testament remains consistent in exalting Jesus as ONE, and yet he is under the Father's will, and led by the power of the Holy Spirit. Jesus works his ONENESS-nature out within the plural nature of a church body with many gifts. We even see a shadow of the Trinity in the Triune offices of the New Testament in the Elder, Deacon, Deaconess model of leadership.

What does this have to do with our healing, the restoration of our leaders, and the betterment of our communities in the Case Study of Chuck and Biblical scenario of King David? The answer to this is very simple. When one person is allowed to sit by their lonesome in the head seat, it's easy to give in to the temptation to be a control freak. Sadly, our current church models actually promote controlling leaders. It's hard to expect that our leaders will act any differently when our environments are actually structured around controlling systems.

We need to lay down our **models** and embrace new **paradigms**. God is three, but One. For good leadership to look like God and act like God, to the best of their abilities, leadership is going to have to be done together. Multiple. Plural. Nowhere in the Bible is there a healthy example of a senior leader up at the top all by themselves. God does his work in teams.

To bring trust back into hurting communities and individuals, and to heal controlling leaders, we need the gospel. In this case, the good news is the Trinity Himself. He's three but ONE. Restructuring our thinking around a paradigm for ministry that allows more than one person to serve amidst accountability to the others, will ensure greater health, safety, and trust for all those involved.

The Gospel Teaches Us to Find Pleasure in Work and Responsibility

In both the story of Chuck and Simon and that of King David, one thing restricted freedom and health from coming into the lives of the leaders and community. That ingredient is Responsibility.

When David took responsibility for his kingdom, he fought alongside his soldiers. He fought for them and for the right reasons. When David stayed back and chose to avoid his responsibility to fight, he got caught in sin, murder, and deception. When both Nathan and Simon took responsibility to stand up for the injustice being caused by their leaders, each of them succeeded in exposing and bringing their leader to justice. If they would have kept silent the cycle would have kept spinning.

Chuck would not take responsibility for his family and his actions, and his sins destroyed all those around him. David would not take responsibility initially for his sins, and it led to the murder of his friend and the sexual assault of his friend's wife.

Responsibility is key. If you think back to Genesis 1 after Adam and Eve disobeyed God by eating of the fruit, God came to the man, the woman, and the serpent to ask who had disobeyed. They all blamed each other. They all pointed their finger at the other person and came up with an excuse why the actions of someone else was worse than their actions.

The saga continues in humanity today. Our sinful nature naturally chooses to take the path of least resistance. We resist courage. We turn our back on true valor. Why? Because it costs us. We dare not suffer. And for those of us who have bought the lie that "we deserve only good things without responsibility," we think we should never have to experience discomfort for any reason—especially if that means we have to embrace hardship for someone else's benefit.

Therefore, to restore fallen leaders and broken communities fleshy pleasures have to be replaced with pleasureless responsibilities (for a season). Healthy responsibility within accountability restores. Let me give you an example.

I remember a well-known evangelist who fell into sexual sin in recent years. His church ousted him, his community condemned him, and his family disowned him. However, a famous preacher (someone you'd know if I named them), called this man up and said, "come to my church, I want to hire you." Obviously, this took the evangelist by surprise, but he asked, "what are the terms?"

The pastor replied, "I want you to come to my church, and for the next year your only job is going to be to share your story. I want you to share your sin and your struggle until it turns sour to you. I want you to share your vices until you speak so repetitively with those who have gone through the same thing that it starts to heal you. In this way, you'll take responsibility for your sin, and you'll see its effects. Through it all, you'll find healing for yourself and for all you've hurt."

There is much wisdom to be gained from the Pastor's response. He knew that reconciliation and true healing would only happen to all involved if pleasureless responsibility came first. And you know what? This evangelist turned his back on his other sexual pleasures through the process because he ended up finding real pleasure. In seeing lives redeemed and people given back their freedom to be honest about their own struggles, he found a deeper joy than he'd ever known. He experienced grace, forgiveness, and mercy at the hands of those he'd offended in such mighty and tangible ways that it trumped any other sensation he'd ever had, or could possibly ever hope to have.

This is how we restore broken people. Not by pleasantry, but with honesty and responsibility.

The Gospel Teaches Us to Release not Restrict

Bad leaders only know restriction and theft. It's the heart of control. In order to get healthy, a bad leader has to walk in the opposite spirit. A person who has known only the restriction and the manipulation that is necessary to preserve one's image and situation must be given opportunities to act contrary to what they have known. For example, the opposite righteous response to one who is filled with greed is to be afforded opportunities to be generous. Acting intentionally in a righteous way that's contrary to the particular sin of struggle is like medication to a sickness. It makes the sick well.

A great case study that helps us understand **restriction** and **release** is in the life of King Herod and King Jesus. Herod (the current king in the time of Jesus) became intimidated when the wise men came looking for the Christ Child. The Scripture says that "he was troubled, and all Jerusalem with him." He entered into competition with Jesus, and this terrorized him so much that he commissioned priests and scribes to search for Jesus under the guise that he too might come and "pay his respects."

Matthew 2:16 clearly reveals the truth of Herod's motives. When the full threat of this baby King of Kings became clear, Herod felt as if he had been tricked, and he "became furious ... and killed all the male children in Bethlehem and in all that region who were two years old or under." His greed produced in him a desire to gather all things to himself and unto his own glory. This desire caused him to restrict anything that stood in his way.

Jesus, on the other hand, in releasing the 12 Apostles in

Matthew 10, "called to him his twelve disciples and gave them authority over unclean spirits, to cast them out, and to heal every disease and every affliction." He commissioned them to go to the lost sheep of Israel and to intentionally forgo any riches of their own. He simply told the Apostles that they had "received without paying" so they must "give without pay." Jesus clearly teaches a system of release.

Notice that he used his authority to empower others. He called people to himself so he could give to them his authority to go and do likewise. Consider also the aim of his empowerment. Any liberation, notoriety, possessions, and esteem given to the disciples by Jesus were used to supply the mission of extending that same freedom to others.

The way to heal broken leaders and communities is to require of those who have played the thief, to go and give—fourfold (Luk. 19:8). Why? Giving is the **righteous act** of release. It heals the **unrighteous action** of restriction. King David and Chuck were consumed with their own name, their own resources, and the preservation of "self." The only thing that is effective in healing an evil stare of selfishness, is to lift our eyes off of ourselves. We must curb our need to control others and to instead turn toward them in an effort to bless them richly.

7 / QUESTIONS FOR DISCUSSION

First, contemplate these questions individually and answer in the space provided. Then join together collectively as a group. Here are some Scriptures that can help guide your discussion:

Verses to Consider: *Jms. 5:16; 1 Tim. 1:12-17; 1 Tim. 2:3-4; 1 Thess. 4:3-8, 5:18; 1 Pet. 5:5-6; Gal. 6:1-5.*

1. What can we do as the Body of Christ to put in place Biblical structures in our homes, families, and churches that provide for greater accountability and vulnerability to those similar to Chuck?

2. How can churches create more "patient, intentional, and slow-moving" structures for people like KJ in order to help them serve and mature, all while receiving the proper guidance and safety to protect them and those they lead?

. . .

3. Chuck often hid behind the mantra "God called me to this." Similarly, many Christians today hide behind phrases like "God spoke to me," or "God gave this to me." Statements like this are very subjective, and people often use them when trying to play off their will as God's will. What results is a lot of false teachings and immorality. What is the believer's responsibility to respond to this type of false teaching and twisting of an implied will of God?

4. Everything comes down to how we as the Body of Christ discern God's voice and calling. How can we as fellow believers understand God's will, and how does Scripture very explicitly tell us what his will is? Is God's will some sort of mystical treasure hunt that we have to discover, or is he gracious enough to give us everything we need to follow his will in his Word?

5. How can we provide the proper balance needed today between what we can control and what we need to constantly surrender?

6. What are some warning signs to watch for in ourselves, and in our brothers and sisters, to assess whether we are becoming like or following a Chuck, a KJ, a Claire, or a Simon?

7. What can we do now in our own lives to address any bitterness or missed expectations—as in the story of King David—that may lead us to commit horrible sins against those we begrudge?

8. It seems odd that King David, a man after God's own heart, didn't even recognize how dark his choices were toward Uriah

until Nathan revealed it to him. Do we take for granted how deceptive sin is in our own lives? How do we remain aware of our sin's constant deceptions in order to avoid falling prey to the same delusions as David?

9. What is the purpose of healthy church families in providing a safe place to share sin, a safe place to heal from sin, and a safe place to be vulnerable and counseled by others in our sin?

10. How can contemplating the Trinity help us put in place better community and leadership structures that require mutual submission and equip people to lead while using their power for the good of the whole?

11. For those who have fallen into very public sin, how can the community rally around them for their good, while also giving offenders pleasure-less responsibilities for a season to restore back to them a heart of service and humility?

12. How can communities put in place righteous action steps for any and all who have fallen into unrighteous patterns of using good things in the wrong ways?

PART 2
CONTRACT OF PERSONALITY VS. COVENANT OF COMMUNITY

8 / THE CASE STUDY

Brilliant. Musical. Savant. Godly.

These words describe Pastor Ty. He's amazing really. When he gets up to speak he's dynamic. Full of personality. He speaks with confidence. He brings to life the Scriptures in his manner of teaching. He's accurate. He's sobering. He's thoughtful and pastoral. His command of God's truth brings a hush of conviction and comfort over the congregation at Hope Church.

He's cordial, warm, and a big hugger off stage. The lights and glamor do not seem to faze him. He runs from the platform regularly like a school child to hug anyone and everyone. He's an unbiased hugger. Children get an embrace. Elderly get a squeeze. He'll lift even the biggest man off his feet.

The church flourishes under his care. It grows far wider than his outstretched arms. In just a little over a month after launching, Hope Church outgrows the cafeteria of a local high school and moves into the gym to support the explosion of excitement.

Kids run everywhere and families change day-by-day into the likeness of Jesus. It's a miracle.

No miracle seems to eclipse Pastor Ty. Take his voice for

instance. When he sings it's like a nightingale. His voice is rich with jazz and crass with the heart of the blues. His proficiency as a music leader is also accompanied by his skill as a jazz pianist. His piano licks and expertise draw out the finest musicians from within the local community. The band hops every Sunday. The music is rich. The experience is grand. Pastor Ty's musicianship inspires the congregation and calls every musician higher in the skill and craft.

In comparison to Ty, no one seems to stand out. That is, except maybe Ray and Timothy. They are light years away from Ty in charisma and talent, but yet they stand closer his equal than anyone else. Ray is an advisor within the church. Not a fellow Pastor, or an equally respected voice to Ty, but wise nonetheless. Ty loves Ray. Timothy oversees the pastoral ministry with the youth. Timothy's energy at reaching youth cannot equal the sheer skill in Ty's many talents, but what Timothy lacks in skill he makes up for in passion and being genuine.

The youth explode in numbers into homes. The church explodes within the gym. Youth break out in Bible studies all over the city. Kids pray for their schools. They see people being saved in droves. It's a revival.

But then ...

Pastor Ty disappears. Like the wind, he blows away quicker than he appeared. Everyone is confused. Everyone looks at each other with the look of deer in headlights. The church that lit up the scene of the local community within just a few short months, now, only six months later, implodes even faster.

Everyone feels lost. People parade around hurt. Their anger, disillusionment, and questions heat up similarly to that of picketers and mobs with lanterns coming to burn someone at the stake. The rhythm in the gym is like a gun waiting to go off.

"Where did he go?" one voice shouts.

"What's going to happen to Hope Church?" another hopelessly gasps.

Ray and Timothy sit in the middle of the room amidst the crowd with empty looks on their faces. Their only answer is "We will try and see what we can find out."

Like a horse out of the gates, Ray and Timothy enlist a team. The first step is to go to Ty's house in order to see if he's still around, or if any of his neighbors can explain the reason why he has vanished. The only problem is, no one in the church knows where Pastor Ty and his family live. No one had ever been to his house. Living in a large town stretching across a huge valley means that there is a lot of terrain to cover in order to try and find him.

Luckily, Ty's wife's cousin lives in town. He had visited the church on opening Sunday, so his address and phone number were on file. The call and visit to his house were made. John, the cousin, indeed knows where the families' house is. But that's all he knows. They are not close. Needless to say, the news that Ty had left surprised him too, but he was more than happy to let the team have the address.

The address to the house lies about a mile away, and yet it feels like it takes an eternity to get there. Driving along, the housing changes from mobile homes and starter houses, into garden homes on small plots of land, and finally into gated mansions in the country. Pastor Ty's house sits majestically on a hill in one of the gated communities. No one can get close to Pastor Ty's house because the gate won't allow it. The only thing the team sees from the edge of the street is a towering mansion with a sign out front that says "SOLD."

As the next few months transpire, Ray and Timothy try their

best to keep Hope Church afloat. But on the very next week, the gym is sparse with only fifteen people. It didn't take more than a few minutes for Hope Church to move into a home in hopes of survival, but it became clear after a few short months that Hope Church was and had been about Pastor Ty. His whole personality had driven the vision and people were there for him. Neither Ray nor Timothy could compete.

It may be safe to assume that the message and life of the gospel really never dwelt at Hope Church. Questions swirled around in the community as to "what we all had been doing in the first place?" Bank records started revealing dollar after dollar that had gone missing. Questions and conspiracy kept mounting. Ray and Timothy were cast as the villains, and within what seemed like the next few minutes, they left as well.

Hope Church ended. Hope Church had been a personality. Hope Church was Pastor Ty. The gospel had been perverted and skewed into worshipping one man, and this one man had embezzled funds, stolen money, lined his pockets with his personality, and to this day no one knows where Pastor Ty ended up.

9 / THE STORY

Obviously, much went wrong in the tragedy of Hope Church. Many reading this book have probably experienced similar failures amongst their leadership within the church, business, community, and otherwise. To some degree, we all can relate, and we all hold our opinionated hurts. However, before we deal with all the colorful abuses in the scenario of Hope Church, let's consider a situation in Scripture that I feel has similar disastrous potential. Joyously, the hero of our story, Ezra, exhibits quite a different pastoral approach.

IMAGINE YOUR LIFE IN CAPTIVITY. Think about what it would feel like to have your practices and your beliefs forbidden under national law. Imagine if your faith automatically placed you in immediate danger under subjection to the tyrannical control of your leader. Add to this fact, that your identity as a people and as a nation no longer exists because you have been completely absorbed by the pagan culture around you.

This is Israel's predicament at the beginning of the book of

Ezra. Because of their sins, God drove them into captivity under the reign of Nebuchadnezzar. They were enslaved in the idolatrous nation of Babylon for 70 years. In Daniel chapter one, we learn that the Babylonians had destroyed the Jewish Temple (the Jews' place of worship and the house of the presence of God), stolen all of its riches and impounded them within the Bank of Babylon, and taken the Israelites as slaves. In Daniel 1:3-7, Nebuchadnezzar took the Jewish youths, who were considered to be the cream-of-the-crop and the up-and-coming leaders of the Israelite nation, and renamed them.

Names in that culture were extremely important. Jewish people would name their children with names that spoke sentences about God's character. Names stated the people's identity. Daniel, whose name means "God is Judge," was renamed Belteshazzar, "Bel will protect," Hananiah, "The LORD is gracious," became Shadrach, meaning "inspired of Aku," Mishael, meaning "Who is like Jehovah," became Meshach, "belonging to Aku," and Azariah, "The LORD is my Help," became Abednego, meaning "servant of Nego." These name changes reveal a glimpse into the mindset and tactics of Nebuchadnezzar. Nebuchadnezzar stripped them of their identity by symbolically dedicating them to his gods. They were lost.

Things weren't getting any better either because we also learn that there was a rising and stronger leader coming quickly in Persia named Cyrus, in the year 536 B.C. Cyrus is heralded in history as being a great leader and decision maker. It was under his own rule that the empire embraced all previous civilized states of the ancient Near East, expanded vastly, and eventually conquered most of Southwest Asia and much of Central Asia from Egypt and the Hellespont in the west to the Indus River in the east, to create the largest empire the world had yet seen.

Negatively, however, Cyrus is also known for resurrecting old cultic high places of worship, and he himself worshipped the god

Marduk. Marduk's deistic qualities were later on connected with water, vegetation, judgment, and magic. Cyrus is also credited with the spread and advancement of the religion of Islam. Cyrus was an extremely powerful, pagan king. The beliefs of his religion were in conflict with the GOD of the Bible—Yahweh.

Nevertheless, Cyrus was part of a bigger plan. God had prophesied through Jeremiah about Cyrus' reign (See Jer. 25:12; 29:10). God spoke about Cyrus through Isaiah some 150 years earlier:

Isaiah 44:28: "It is I who says of Cyrus, 'He is My shepherd! And he will perform all My desire.' And he declares of Jerusalem, 'She will be built,' and of the temple, 'Your foundation will be laid.'"

Isaiah 45:1: "Thus says the LORD to Cyrus His anointed, whom I have taken by the right hand, to subdue nations before him And to loose the loins of kings; To open doors before him so that gates will not be shut."

Isaiah 45:12: "It is I who made the earth and created man upon it. I stretched out the heavens with My hands and I ordained all their host."

Cyrus was used by God to release Israel from captivity to go back to Jerusalem in order to rebuild their temple and their city. Many chosen leaders were wrapped up in the aftermath of the rebuilding of the temple and the wall surrounding Jerusalem: Nehemiah, Zerubbabel, and the prophets Haggai, Zechariah, and one could even say, Malachi. However, the pastoral or priestly figure that worked his way into the culture in many of the most transforming ways after they returned back to Jerusalem from exile out of Babylon was Ezra.

Ezra is a leader that lies in deep, deep, contrast to that of

Nebuchadnezzar in particular. He is a servant. His posture of humility lies in stark contrast to the prideful arrogance of Nebuchadnezzar. The "cult of personality" surrounding the narcissism of Nebuchadnezzar had imprisoned and broken the Jewish people for years. These leaders attempted to steal Israel's identity, their riches, their communal unity, and their dignity. Into this context God used Ezra.

WE NOW JUMP some twenty-three years into the future after the exiles came back to rebuild the temple and the wall around Jerusalem. The temple is completed. Nebuchadnezzar and Cyrus are gone, and Artaxerxes has been King in Persia for seven years. In Ezra 7:6 we are told that Ezra is sent to the people because "he was a scribe skilled in the Law of Moses that the Lord, the God of Israel, had given, and the king granted him all that he asked for the hand of the Lord his God was on him."

Ezra was given the rights by King Artaxerxes to replenish Israel's wealth and supply (9:21-24), to elect judges and political officials (9:25), and to teach the Law of God to the people (9:26). He was also allowed to restore the priestly work in the temple (9:15-36). To such a glorious miracle, Ezra responds in 9:27-28 with these words:

> Blessed be the Lord, the God of our fathers, who put such a thing as this into the heart of the king, to beautify the house of the Lord that is in Jerusalem, and who extended to me his steadfast love before the king and his counselors, and before all the king's mighty officers. I took courage, for the hand of the Lord my God was on me, and I gathered leading men from Israel to go up with me.

Everything up to this point in Ezra's story is nothing short of supernatural. God was taking care of his people, but in Ezra 9-10, we come to a bit of a climax in the story. A big problem appears.

While in Captivity, God's people had intermarried with people from pagan nations. This is something they were explicitly told by God to never do. Upon hearing this, Ezra blushes in embarrassment (9:6), tears his clothes and pulls out his beard in repentance (9:3), and rises at the evening sacrifice to spread out his hands before the people in a prayer to God:

O my God, I am ashamed and blush to lift my face to you, my God, for our iniquities have risen higher than our heads, and our guilt has mounted up to the heavens. From the days of our fathers to this day we have been in great guilt. And for our iniquities we, our kings and our priests, have been given into the hand of the kings of the lands, to the sword, to captivity, to plundering, and to utter shame, as it is today. But now for a brief moment favor has been shown by the Lord our God, to leave us a remnant and to give us a secure hold within his holy place, that our God may brighten our eyes and grant us a little reviving in our slavery. For we are slaves. Yet our God has not forsaken us in our slavery but has extended to us his steadfast love before the kings of Persia, to grant us some reviving to set up the house of our God, to repair its ruins, and to give us protection in Judea and Jerusalem.

And now, O our God, what shall we say after this? For we have forsaken your commandments, which you commanded by your servants the prophets, saying, "The land that you are entering, to take possession of it, is a land impure with the impurity of the peoples of the lands, with their abominations that have filled it from end to end with their uncleanness. Therefore do not give your daughters to their sons, neither take their daughters for your sons and never seek their peace or prosperity, that you may be strong and eat the good of the land and leave it for an inheritance to your children forever." And after all that has come upon us for our evil deeds and for our great guilt, seeing that you, our God, have punished us less than our iniquities deserved and have given us such a remnant as this, shall we break your commandments again and intermarry with the peoples who practice these abominations? Would you not be angry with us until you consumed us so that there should be no remnant, nor any to escape? O Lord, the God of Israel, you are just, for we are left a remnant that has escaped, as it is today. Behold, we are before you in our guilt, for none can stand before you because of this.

Israel had come to this place of compromise very slowly. Creeping in, evil overtook them. They no longer considered things to be evil that the Lord had declared evil. They had been so hood-winked and hazed by their leaders in Babylon, that they could not even understand a Biblical way of life anymore.

10 / THE SIN

You may be wondering if there's any comparison to be made between the story of Ezra and the situation with Pastor Ty. Alas, there's much to learn. I'd like us to see the havoc that was caused amongst God's people in both situations when the cult of celebrity took over. In our Biblical story, Nebuchadnezzar is a prime example of a man who puts himself in the seat of God. In doing so, he displaces God's people, strips them of identity, tatters their ability to trust, and deluges them with waves of disunity and fragmentation. He forced people to become idol worshippers.

Turning men and women into idols to be worshipped is nothing new to humanity or to the church. Long after the events in Ezra, the Corinthian church was a church full of people looking to make an idol out of something or somebody. In chapter one of 1 Corinthians, Paul identifies a few types of Christians that were emerging. For brevity's sake, we will refer to these developing Christian-flavored-people as the star-struck (1:10-17), the stoic (1:20), the debater (1:20), the Jew and the Greek (1:22), and the nobleman believer (1:26). The star-struck Christians were making celebrities out of the Apostles. Some of them were following

Paul, others Cephas, and others Apollos. Rather than welcoming the hero worship from these people, however, Paul responds; "Is Christ divided? Was Paul crucified for you? Or were you baptized in the name of Paul?" Paul's point: "Why are you putting people on a pedestal?"

There were also those perceived as "wise" Christians. These were the stoics. They were the sober-minded ones because they believed that emotions are destructive. The greater body of Stoics, the Epicureans, particularly thought themselves astute in the debate of God and human suffering. They were a dismal crowd. They walked around talking about how God either can and won't heal suffering, wants to and can't, can't and won't, or won't and can't heal suffering.

The Scribes were the educated lawyers. The debaters were akin to modern-day bloggers, tabloids, T.V., reporters, and advertisements. The Jews would only believe if they saw signs and wonders, and the Greeks would only believe if they were provided fact and proof. Finally, was the nobleman. They were the prosperity Christians—believing that health, wealth, and prosperity were the name of the game.

What results from the cult of celebrity is division and all shapes and sizes of heresy. Exalting personalities develops in us a mindset of **contract** not one of **covenant.** Contractual thinking is the real root sin and the drastic effect lying sneakily behind the actions of Pastor Ty and kings like Nebuchadnezzar. Contracts are based on rules. If you keep the rules, the contract stands. If the rules are broken, so is the commitment. For example, if someone signs a contract with a credit card company and fails to pay, that credit card company doesn't care what happens to the debtor. They'll take their house, their finances, and everything the family calls their own until the debt is paid back. Covenant is the opposite. It's based on loyalty to that which is unbreakable. Covenant is a biblical idea that God forges with his people. God remains steadfast in his commitment to his people no matter the circumstances. His connection to us is not based on our effort to keep the rules, but about his faithfulness and desire for our good.

What Nebuchadnezzar and Pastor Ty did equally was to forge a contract with God's people. That contract stated that they would **use** people rather than **serve** them until all they needed was satisfied. Bottom line, contracts always have endings, covenants do not. In Nebuchadnezzar's case, God ended him by taking his reign away and confronting and redeeming him (Dan. 4). Lucky Nebuchadnezzar. In Pastor Ty's case, we don't really know the whole story. The assumption can possibly be made that his fraud concerning money was about to be made public so he ended things. We might also assume that he had already taken enough money to meet his needs and was ready to move on. Whatever the case, he entered Hope Church with a contract mindset, and with stipulations that served only his interest. He "loved" the people until that interest was met. Then he bailed.

Real love never happened in either case.

It's not a surprise that the "Ezras" are left to pick up the pieces left by the Tys of the world. In both cases—with Hope Church and with the Israelites—the people were the ones left holding the bag. Not only had they been hurt and left bewildered, but they too had become a **contract** people. In Hope Church's case, everyone simply left. Their quick exodus proves why they were there in the first place. It's clear they never understood covenant. In Ezra's case, contract had formed all the same but it outfitted itself through a slightly different deformed community.

In Ezra 9-10 we are given a glimpse into a huge scene of repentance concerning **inter-marriage**. The reason marriage is singled out in Ezra is because it was set up by God to be a covenant relationship, not a contract. A covenant is an agreement made between two people to commit to each other for life ... for better or for worse; until death do us part. In covenant, two people commit to follow God as their leader, and they commit to love each other the best they know how. Marriage is the most profound picture of **covenant commitment** in the Bible.

Intermarriage breaks this image of covenantal love—and when I speak of intermarrying, I'm NOT speaking of marriages forged between two different races or people of differing cultures. The type of intermarrying the book of Ezra has in mind is the intertwining of different faiths. 2 Corinthians 6:14 says it this way, "Do not be yoked together with unbelievers. For what do righteousness and wickedness have in common? Or what fellowship can light have with darkness?" A yoke is a piece of wood or a binding mechanism that holds two oxen together as they pull a wagon. If the oxen are the same size, the binding is level and each ox can offer equal pulling strength to the load, but if one ox is sick or smaller than the other oxen, then the yoke will be unequal. The unevenness will cause stress, burden, and angst on the stronger animal, as he/she has to pull the other one.

Intermarrying is an act of unequal yoking. God calls us to eat, walk with, befriend, and love the lost, but not to bind ourselves to them in covenant or in close accountable relationships. The world operates by different standards, and they don't follow Jesus nor do they know him. To bind ourselves to unbelievers via a loan, a marriage, a vow, a lease, or a business contract is unwise. I Corinthians 15:33 says "Do not be misled: 'Bad company corrupts good character.'"

The Israelites disobeyed God's command in Deuteronomy that directed them not to marry men and women from other faiths; which in the time of Ezra was also predominantly represented by other cultures. God's Deuteronical decree was not given to ruin the Israelites' fun. It was a law made in love to help them. God knew that if the Israelites bound themselves in contract to nonbelievers, negative influence would follow.

When we, in like manner to the Israelites, begin to partner and bind ourselves to the world, the cause and effect prescribed in I Corinthians begins to take place. We become more like the world. This is the sin of Israel in the day of Ezra. This is the sin of Hope Church. This is the sin that lies deep in the heart of every human. Without God, we are a **contractual people,** not **covenantal.**

11 / THE PSYCHOLOGY (PERSONAL PAIN & MOTIVE)

Living contractually develops in us the following psychological traits: self-entitlement, self-interest, hatred towards people, and narcissism. Let's look at all of these in the context of contractual marriage, since this seems to be the symbolic context of Ezra and what God addresses in Israel.

For example, when some couples get married today, they sign a contract detailing what each party is going to do and be in the marriage. The marriage contract is accompanied by prenups, pre-expectations, and by-laws for each partner to follow. These guidelines are added as protective mechanisms in the relationship. These "safety measures" are tools of distrust. They are put in place to ensure that if one partner doesn't keep their end of the bargain, the other spouse can contractually divorce them because the terms have been breached. It's a business, not a marriage. It's selfish and not servant-hearted.

Self-preservation mechanisms are not only present in prenup situations, but in the way most people approach relationships in general. Our world today is filled with a mentality of divorce, giving up, friends with benefits, falling out of love, and leaving for a variety of reasons and on a variety of levels. Consider how contractual poisons make their way in. In a contractual outlook, each party in any kind of relationship maintains a position of being self-entitled. An unspoken expectation exists that they are going to be perfectly loved or else the deal is off. Ironically, even an idiot can see that this will never work because humans aren't perfect. Humans let each other down by mistakes and naturally tend to protect themselves from suffering rather than embrace difficulty. Contracts hold off the goodness that comes to us through difficulty, mistakes, failing forward, and learning our way through life together. Contracts kill growth. It provokes entitlement. The two people who enter the contract are actually ensuring that they will **never become better people.** Ironically enough, our betterment is actually one of God's primary reasons for relationships in the first place.

Any mentality that screams "leave me the way that I am" sets both parties up for disaster. Losing interest in the true betterment of the other person violates the essential ingredient for love. The spiral of self-centered interest dooms those in relationship to hate each other—hate being to deprive each other of love. Once a culture of withdrawing and attack sets in, each wrong offense is interpreted as a breach in contract. It's viewed as an intentional wound to the other's psyche and identity. The pain brought on by the other is no longer perceived as an accident, a mistake, or as a sin that can be forgiven and reconciled. Each mistake is a reason to hate and ultimately disconnect from the other person.

The conclusion? A full blown narcissist forms. Divorce happens. Separation. Leaving. Isolation. A narcissist is a person who seeks a world that revolves around them. Me. Myself. I. It's self-worship. It's idolatry of the highest kind, and the Bible says it leads to all kinds of evil. Once a person starts living in **contract** over **covenant**, any attempts at glorifying God are lost. The person seeks only to glorify self, and as Scripture tells us, to make much of one's self will only lead to a dissatisfied soul, not a joyous one.

12 / COMMUNITY PAIN & MOTIVE

It's not hard to imagine what a "marriage-mentality-of-contract" can do to a family, a community, a city, a culture, and the world surrounding it. Contracts birth nothing but division and pain. I apologize for being a Debbie-downer in continuing on here, but we need to see the absolute heartbreak that contract causes. In Ezra 10:2-4a we see the consequences:

> We have broken faith with our God and have married foreign women from the peoples of the land, but even now there is hope for Israel in spite of this. Therefore let us make a covenant with our God to put away all these wives and their children, according to the counsel of my lord and of those who tremble at the commandment of our God, and let it be done according to the Law. Arise, for it is your task.

Contract is practice for Divorce. It's practice for an ultimate parting of ways. Doing things our own way, for our own pleasure, and in a way that leaves us as the center is setting us up for heartbreak. Look at what happens in Ezra's day. Children lose their Daddies. Wives lose their husbands. People are forced to deal with deep physical, emotional, mental, and spiritual pain. Contract breaks things.

This is the result we see in marriages of contract today. Division. Hatred. We see the percentages for divorced families skyrocketing. Broken and blended families are becoming "normal." Kids are left with no home—being forced to tell people where they stay, not where they live. Out billows more distrust. The story only gets worse. These deadened kids grow up to do dead things. Disconnection and low commitment level rise in the workforce. Contracts skyrocket in finance, business, and any matter where two or more entities come together. Young adults in personal relationships hide behind apps like Tinder to hook up sexually with people in an attempt to avoid the risk of ever being known. It's a way to get what one wants without having to face consequences. Using and abusing someone for one's own gratification is just a click away. We live in a world of **hidden contracts.** People are on the loose looking for what will advance them, what will make their name great, and what will feed their lust, etc. From our self-seeking attitude springs murder, rape, violence, slander, gossip, and every kind of evil one can imagine.

And where did all this start? Well, in our scenario, it began in the heart of one "anti-God" leader who chose to do things for himself. Out of Nebuchadnezzar and Pastor Ty came destruction for everyone else.

13 / THE REMEDY

We can learn much about the remedy to our Case Study and biblical story that is pleasantly helpful from Ezra. Ezra's actions in Chapters 9-10 are instructive for our full recovery, reconciliation, and re-awakening in the aftermath of our own entitlement. Ezra presents a picture of a "good leader." Considering how he handles the situation may help leaders avoid becoming Pastor Tys, and it will help communities to remain safe from being duped by them. Considering Ezra's response will also help those messed over by the "Tys" of the world, to react in ways healthier than just calling it quits. This helps no one.

Ezra's countercultural approach is helpful in our world today as many are dealing with Nebuchadnezzar-type leaders who oppress them, take advantage of them for their own gain, and even kill anyone not aligned with them. Many reading this book serve, have served, or will serve under entitled, narcissistic, selfish, "my vision," leaders. Sadder still, we all in some manner have become like Israel, in that we have embraced **hidden contracts** in the way we think about a variety of relationships. We've developed our own set of rules that come with us everywhere we go. We carry our own baggage, our own guidelines, and our own expectations for how we will be treated.

But to heal …

To really heal …

To truly move from **selfish** to **servant** …

We need the gospel.

In Ezra 9-10 we see hope emerge through the fog. We see the gospel. We see glimpses of healing. We see the great heart of a priest and a pastor who intercedes for his followers and those in sin around him. In seeing how he confesses and repents of the sin of Israel as well as his own sin, we can learn the difference between godly sorrow and mere human apology. Ezra takes to heart the sin of his nation and how they'd turned from God, and he makes a spectacle of himself.

First, Conviction (vs. 3-4)

We see Ezra's honest-to-goodness recognition of his sin. His deep conviction has only to do with how his and the people's relationship with Yahweh have been hindered. His first reaction is not to point fingers at anyone in the situation. His first reaction is to ask himself, "How could I have done this?" Add to his healthy introspection a conviction and true desire to see all wrongs righted. He doesn't wallow in condemnation, self-pity, or worldly guilt. These things only lead to more depression and worldly sorrow. Ezra lets this offense sit deep inside.

Ezra feels the weight of his people's transgressions against God. Ultimately all sin is against God. All our efforts made in shame and trickery are at their base a slam against God's perfect order. That's why Jesus had to come and die on a cross. Jesus had to fulfill all righteousness. Perfection. He had to right our vile nature from the moment we emerged from the womb. We begin life by yelling at our moms for milk, and so Jesus was born of a virgin so that he could right our wrongs from the cradle onward. Our sin is vile. It's a stench to God. When we are truly convicted of our sin, there's a deep realization that what we've done has broken the heart of JESUS.

Second, Confession (vs. 6-7)

Ezra confesses the sins of the people. Does he confess to God because God doesn't know what the people did? NO! God knows. Confession serves us more than it serves God. By confessing, we agree in our hearts with God that our action is in fact sin. We name our sin. In the case of Pastor Ty, the sin of the people was idolatry. They prized a man more than God. It led to deception and confusion. Ty just took advantage of it.

All of us bring real offenses before God that need forgiveness. Nebuchadnezzar confessed his. Ezra confessed his. Pastor Ty needed to confess his. Hope Church needed to confess theirs. We all need to confess. We're all in this together! We can't leave each other. We need to do this together.

The Bible tells us that if we confess our sins, God is faithful and just to forgive us. Ezra is a man who understands the healing power of confession. He names Israel's sins with exactness and doesn't try and conceal anything. He knows that confession brings healing (James 5:16).

Third, Credit (vs. 8-9)

Ezra immediately attributes any good or grace in the situation to God. He praises God for past events where God delivered them from bondage, and he credits God with not leaving them or forsaking them. In the midst of sin, Ezra takes credit for sin and places it on his own head, and any grace and mercy given to the Israelites in spite of their ugliness, he CREDITS to God. God's action is always to demonstrate grace, faithfulness, and forgiveness to those who will repent. Ezra recognizes man's faults as the sole source of separation between each other and our gracious God. James 1:13 says, "When tempted, no one should say, 'God is tempting me.' For God cannot be tempted by evil, nor does he tempt anyone." Ezra fully realizes that it is not God that causes anyone to sin, but people do wrong things all by themselves.

Fourth, Repentance (vs. 14)

Ezra makes a statement of repentance: "… shall we again break your [God's] commandments and intermarry?" His heart is sorrowful not just because they get **caught** in sin by God, but that they had tried to **cover** it up. He does his due diligence to make sure that this mistake would not be made again on his watch. Ezra's confession is followed by action. It's a complete change of mind and heart. In the New Testament, this is referred to as repentance. It is a gift God gives. God allows Israel to repent and to change their minds about their actions, and he points them in a different direction.

Ezra's cycle is the ONLY formula that works for growth in covenant and authentic transformation. ***God looks for honest conviction, coupled with confession of sin, that results in giving credit to God for his mercy and grace***. Simple.

Ezra's repentance is loud, obnoxious, and vocal. As a leader of his community, he sets an example of humility, brokenness, and authenticity. He takes responsibility for the direct sins in his community that he himself does not commit. Not many leaders or pastors stand wailing and ripping their clothes over the sins of the people and our world. Maybe they should. People in the world need to see this attitude on display in us. If we carry ourselves with entitlement, arrogance, narcissism, and self-interest, and continue to live in sin just like everyone else, then we are not modeling and imitating Christ. As leaders, we should be helping all those around us to welcome this posture of worship. A posture of surrender and brokenness. God broke Ezra. God's heavy hand impaled Ezra as if on a stake of conviction, and he let it work him over before he worked over his followers. This is godly leadership that is worth emulating.

14 / QUESTIONS FOR DISCUSSION

First, contemplate these questions individually and answer in the space provided, and then join together collectively as a group. Here are some Scriptures that can help guide your discussion:

Verses to Consider: *1 Cor. 1:10-18; Ez. 10; Gal. 6:9; Jms. 1:12; Rom. 5:3-5; Acts 2:42.*

1. Many today hold to a caricature of glitz and glam regarding what a church or Pastor has to possess to be an acceptable church. If Paul were alive today, would he recognize the way in which we "do church?" Why or why not?

2. In I Corinthians, many were following Paul. Many were following Peter. Many were following Apollos. The cult of personality and the cult of Christian celebrity has always been a

problem in the church. How do we work today in our own homes and the way we live life to deal with the tendency to think too much of ourselves?

3. What are some things we can look for in ourselves to evaluate whether we are seeking to use people for our purposes or serve them for their good?

4. Talk through how Ezra handled the situation after the Exile. How should this instruct us in our responsibilities as the family of God today? How should this instruct how we see the role of our Pastors?

5. When you assess your own life, do you see evidence that you are becoming more of a contract person or a covenantal one? What kinds of things can we commit to as God's family so that we become covenantal people?

6. What are some ways you see hidden contracts in our world, culture, church, and family life today?

7. What is the church's role in making us better people while we walk together along the road of God's sanctification? How has today's church-hopping and no-loyalty culture actually kept communities and people from becoming better?

. . .

8. If you have fallen, or know others who have fallen prey to similar situations and sins as found in the scenario of Ezra or Pastor Ty, how do you practically act out some of the gospel remedies provided in this chapter?

PART 3
CHIEFS & INDIANS

15 / THE CASE STUDY

Reared as a Quaker, Herbert W. Armstrong joined the Oregon Conference of the Church of God in the late 1920s and by 1931 was ordained as one of its ministers. Armstrong founded the Radio Church of God in 1934, broadcasting his prophecy-oriented "The World Tomorrow" program from Eugene, Oregon. He began publishing *The Plain Truth* as a mimeographed newsletter.

After World War II Armstrong moved his headquarters to Pasadena, California. He adopted the name Worldwide Church of God in 1968 and WWCG quickly became known for an assortment of doctrinal distinctives that were open heresies toward biblical truth. Among other aberrations, Armstrong:

- Condemned the Trinity as a pagan doctrine.
- Taught that "all saints" become little gods after their resurrection.
- Denied that Christians can be born again prior to the resurrection.
- Promoted Anglo-Israelism, the belief that British

people are the literal descendants of the ten lost tribes of Israel.
- Urged keeping the Old Testament law, including strict Sabbath observance and dietary restrictions.
- Prohibited celebrating Christmas or Easter, which he condemned as pagan holidays. (Instead, WWCG members observed seven Holy Days: Passover, the Festival of Unleavened Bread, Pentecost, the Festival of Trumpets, the Day of Atonement, the Festival of Tabernacles, and the Last Great Day.)
- Forbade members to consult medical doctors when sick.
- Stressed tithing as a legalistic extreme. (Strictly observant WWCG members gave 30 percent: 10 percent for a regular tithe, 10 percent to support the annual Feast of Tabernacles, and 10 percent intended to support widows and orphans within the WWCG)
- Forbade members to remarry after divorce and insisted that they remain celibate if they remarried after divorce.
- Insisted that the WWCG was the only true church.
- Closed the movement's doors to visitors and welcomed only converts.

Following in step with wild false teachings were accusations of sexual misconduct. In 1971, Armstrong's handsome son and heir-apparent, Garner Ted, was relieved of his WWCG duties, reinstated, then relieved of his duties again. In 1978 Garner Ted Armstrong founded the Church of God International, a movement he led until November 1995, when a lawsuit charging him with sexual assault caused him to step down.

Armstrong appointed Joseph W. Tkach as director of church administration in 1979, and Tkach soon began dismantling the authoritarian structure in local congregations. He also began noticing that much of their teaching at WWCG was absolute untruthful and not in line with the Bible. This led to a revival of many sorts in the WWCG; doctrinal, structural, and otherwise. WWCG leadership approached many godly men for help in their reformation and biblical learning. One of the people they consulted was Hank Hanegraaf. Hank reflects on their reform as a miracle: "This is unprecedented in church history. It's the very kind of thing that those who have given their lives in ministry to the kingdom of the cults hope for."[1]

Up from the settling ashes of reformation and revival within the cult of The Worldwide Church of God rose Salvation Church. Led by beloved Pastor, Rex Riddle.

Pastor Rex is quiet. Gentle. He listens. He's unassuming, docile, and one might almost miss him in a room. In his gentleness is the strength of Jesus. His gentleness is humility. He carries the torch of the "new way" for the WWCG, and his congregation listens to him. Though a road full of hard suffering and re-learning lay in Rex's path, the people trust Rex. He's courageous. They see him as willing to take upon himself the difficult task of leading himself and others out of drastically false teaching.

Rex is also a great listener. Having the skill to listen well helps when trying to understand people's false beliefs in order to lead them to the truth. However, he's perhaps too good a listener. He's skilled in making others feel heard, but not in helping people weigh their own words in light of truth. He is shy in the face of confrontation. He exhorts people, but fails to admonish or rebuke them. On one hand, his willingness to consider the questions and hurts of the others in the WWCG movement helps them to openly process their paradigm shift and their disillusionment amidst all the changes. He stabilizes people. But on the other hand, he fails to hold them accountable to the Word of God in calling them to action and repentance.

Many in the WWCG movement require both a listening ear and deep admonishment and teaching. Their questions need real answers. Though over time, they slowly arrive at truth in thought, their methods in how to "do church" remain cultic. Largely, they are still unchanged.

Nothing quite reveals that little has changed in the minds of the former WWCG church members than when Rex has to step down because his day job requires him and his family to move overseas. Rex is heartbroken, and yet faces the reality that he now has to release his congregation of just a little over two hundred congregants into the hands of new leadership. He cannot be there to listen anymore. He is forced to leave for the good of his family and the provisions of his job as a bi-vocational Pastor. In putting into place of process of stepping aside as leader, Rex realizes something fairly tragic. His little Indians have become so dependent on their chief, that they cannot make decisions on their own.

Fast forward ... Rex is now two weeks gone, and already there are many in the church angling for power. One group wants to search for a new Pastor, one group elects a man already there in the congregation, and one small sect wants to lead the small church back into the foundational teachings of WWCG. The cult mentality surfaces. The questions come: "Did anyone really buy into and believe their teachings were false and the Bible is true?" This people, a people that had been trained to blindly follow orders, lost a leader. A people calibrated to follow control and abuses of power now suddenly had power handed to them with little idea how to wield the sword.

Under Rex's leadership the people were allowed to have a heavy voice. They demanded to be listened to. This is all well and good when there's accountable leadership in place to direct demands toward God-glorifying ends. However, when left alone to questions, riots, and differing opinions, people carrying a heavy voice, with no understanding of authority, turn good into chaos.

In the case of Salvation Church, the questions turn to demands. Rights! The opinions expressed in conversation change to dogmatism, religion, and rules strictly enforced. These people were never taught to do things on their own (to fish for themselves, as the age old analogy goes), and when left without safety and sense of control, all hell broke loose. Sadly, divisions overtook Salvation Church, and she crumbles amidst a sea of hurt feelings, disillusionment, and pride.

---

[1] LeBlanc, D. *The Worldwide Church of God: Resurrected into Orthodoxy.* http://www.equip.org/article/the-worldwide-church-of-god-resurrected-into-orthodoxy/. (Accessed May 17, 2017).

There are many factors to consider in the case study of Salvation Church. Pondering the situation can lead to some real fruit and understanding in our life concerning power, leadership, our own voice, and more. However, let's first consider a story in the Bible of a similar flavor. In doing so, we may just be able to see that the problem of Salvation Church is really not new at all. It's a normal occurrence for those that forget God as their leader.

WHAT HAPPENED in our Case Study is exactly what happened in the times of the Judges. From the conquest of Canaan by Joshua up until the formation of the first Kingdom of Israel and Judah (ca. 1150–1025 BC), the Israelite tribes formed a loose confederation. No central government existed in this confederation. In times of crisis, the people were led by ad hoc chieftains, known as judges."[1]

During the time of the judges, a vicious oppressive cycle crept in and began to repeat itself. First, a leader and people would sin and fall into idolatry. Second, this led to the nation of Israel being oppressed by other nations, abused under the control of their falsely religious king, and/or led astray under the rule, restriction, and demands of their false gods. Third, the people would eventually erupt in pleas for help, deliverance, and repentance, and the graciousness of the Lord would respond in delivering them unto salvation. Finally, and lastly, they would rest.

The people's rest was always short-lived, regrettably. Though the Lord provided sweet deliverance to his people often under a new judge—a leader who honored God—the people and the new leadership would drift toward sin and idolatry once again and the whole process would start over. The cycle of sin in Judges continued on even into the rule of Samuel, the final Judge.

Samuel was a quiet man. Docile. Obedient. Gentle. He was the son of Hannah. His mother had been barren for many years and had prayed for the Lord to give her a son. When Samuel was finally born, she was so thankful for him that she dedicated him to the temple of God to serve as a priest under the oversight of Eli.

Samuel was faithful. He was a good man who submitted willingly to Eli. Sadly, Eli and his household became increasingly more wicked over the course of time. Eli's sons were wicked. They fell under false teachings. They defiled the temple. They disobeyed the Lord, and the Lord rejected Eli's household because of the wickedness of his sons (1 Sam. 2:12-36).

The Lord called Samuel out after the fall of Eli's family. God made Samuel not only a Judge (a king), and a Priest, but he now commissioned Samuel to be a Prophet. He was known among the people as a voice, or a "sent one." He was commissioned with the task of taking people through false teaching into a vibrant relationship with God and his truth.

The Lord told Samuel: "Behold, I am about to do a thing in Israel at which the two ears of everyone who hears it will tingle. On that day I will fulfill against Eli all that I have spoken concerning his house, from beginning to end. And I declare to him that I am about to punish his house forever, for the iniquity that he knew, because his sons were blaspheming God, and he did not restrain them. Therefore I swear to the house of Eli that the iniquity of Eli's house shall not be atoned for by sacrifice or offering forever" (1 Sam. 3:12-14). From the point God spoke to Samuel onward, Samuel grew and the Lord was with him. The Lord did not let one of Samuel's words fall to the ground in a lack of truth and integrity (1 Sam. 3:19). The Lord filled Samuel with the truth. The Scriptures tell us that his call and influence were universal throughout Israel. All of Israel, "from Dan to Beersheba, knew that Samuel was established as a prophet of the Lord" (vs. 20).

Samuel spoke confidently. He was a generous leader. He was kind. He was also ruthless toward all the false teaching and idol worship that had crept into Israelite practice. In Samuel 7:3-4, Samuel said to the people, "'If you are returning to the Lord with all your hearts, then rid yourselves of the foreign gods and the Ashtoreths and commit yourselves to the Lord and serve him only, and he will deliver you out of the hand of the Philistines.' So the Israelites put away their Baals and Ashtoreths, and served the Lord only." The people obeyed. The people listened. Samuel listened, and as a result, unity to some degree became reality in Israel. However, like with any great story, or any great hero, things always come to an end. Despite all of Samuel's success as a leader, the end of his life reads much the same as that of Eli or anyone else. In 1 Samuel 8:1-4 the Scriptures tell us:

> When Samuel became old, he made his sons judges over Israel. The name of his firstborn son was Joel, and the name of his second, Abijah; they were judges in Beersheba. Yet his sons did not walk in his ways but turned aside after gain. They took bribes and perverted justice. Then all the elders of Israel

gathered together and came to Samuel at Ramah and said to him, "Behold, you are old and your sons do not walk in your ways. Now appoint for us a king to judge us like all the nations." But the thing displeased Samuel when they said, "Give us a king to judge us."

We all know the story, God finally did give the people their king. Saul. But we also know that God gave the people Saul not out of excitement to meet the people's needs, but out of great sadness. Like a parent who allows their child to finally touch a scalding burner after many failed attempts to get the child to obey, God allowed Israel to touch what he knew would not satisfy them. He allowed hurt to enter in order to discipline them. He allowed the experience to become their teacher in order that they may come back to the truth that he himself is the true King.

All in all, one fact in particular links the story of Samuel with that of Rex's situation. Both leaders led people who were being brought out of false teachings. But the people were never learning. The people failed to develop their own convictions despite their teacher's efforts, and it begs the question to us, "Are we contributing to this same thing today?"

---

[1] Kitchens, K. A. *On The Reliability of the Old Testament* (Grand Rapids, MI: William B. Eerdmans, 2003).

17 / THE SIN

How then should we compare the Case Study of Rex Riddle and The Worldwide Church of God to that of Samuel and the plight of the Israelites? What is their sin? What's the underlying germ to the symptoms? In both cases, the heart is revealed in the wake of absent leadership and in the presence of abusive leadership.

In both stories, the root sin plaguing every heart is the effort to **find a God-substitute.** Idolatry. Misplaced worship. Broken honor. Allegiance given to the wrong object. Those in the WWCG paid greater honor to their cultic leaders than to the words of their honest God. They blindly and willfully followed in the steps of leaders that fashioned for them a false picture of God. When the WWCG experienced their revival the idolatrous posture of the people turned to follow Rex Riddle. Though his intentions were restorative and every attempt he made was for the good of their healing, the people over-prized him all the same. When Rex was taken away to go overseas, the people responded very similarly to that of Israelites in the wake of Samuel: "Give us a king to judge us."

Israel over-prized their godly servant in the form of Samuel, and their idolatry erupted when Samuel came to his death bed. The people gave in to fear. 1 Samuel 8:7-9 tells us that the whole reason that the people sought for themselves a new King was out of fear. In their fear, they rejected the Lord.

Curious isn't it? The want of **no shepherd**—anarchy—and the want of **control**—top-heavy government—stems from the same root. Fear. The WWCG was the people's god, and it failed them. Rex became their god, and he too failed them. Samuel was held in high esteem amongst the Israelites and yet they prized him too highly. He became in their hearts a god, and he too failed them. Some people cried out "Let's go back to the old system." Some said, "Let's get ourselves a new leader, and fast." Tragically, no one ever uttered, "We are safe … the Lord is our King … let's trust him."

What results in both scenarios is ill-equipped and insecure people who lack the ability to govern themselves. In part, the responsibility in this tragedy falls on the people for being so ignorant and dependent, and yet we also must cast some of the sins onto Rex and Samuel. In Rex's case, he listened, and yet never admonished. He never taught. He never trained. He heard, but he never challenged. He discussed the wrong truths that were believed, but never commanded the people with God's authority to repent of their wrong thinking. The worship shift never happened. Rex failed to help the people learn the truth for themselves. He spoon-fed them the truth as milk, but never pressed them to eat meat. To chew. To grind down on tough questions in the search for one's own convictions. This is a different teaching style altogether.

To require people to do their own chewing is the way of Jesus. Consider this fact: for every "one" statement made by Jesus in the gospels, he asks "four" questions. Striking really. A 4:1 ratio. Jesus modeled for us an altogether different way of discipleship. His way of teaching is almost foreign to our modern day ways of monologue preaching and is much more closely related to what Proverbs 20:5 says, "The purposes of a person's heart are deep waters, but one who has insight draws them out." Jesus didn't just tell people the truth, but he led them in a process of their own discovery. Through question. Through parable. **He didn't fish for them, he taught them how to fish. He didn't teach them what to think, but how to learn.**

Jesus equips his family with the tools, paradigms, and principles that they need in order to conduct their own life affairs. He doesn't do the work for us. He does the work in and through us. Big difference.

In both Rex's case and Samuel's case we see failure in the people, but perhaps a similar failure in the leadership as well. Rex failed to equip the people with the tools to digest the truth. We see that Samuel failed to pass on the truths of God to his own kids. Somewhere along the line, his sons never learned the values of the priesthood, nor the heart of service to the Lord. We know that to some degree it is the parent's responsibility to pass on truth and service to the Lord. This is why parents are held to a higher standard. This is why James 3:1 says that very few should actively desire to **teach** or to **equip** others, "knowing that we shall receive the greater judgment." Those who actively leave behind a legacy, particularly in what they teach or fail to teach, do not get a free pass. They're accountable. The Rexes and the Samuels of world history are accountable in a manner possibly higher than even that of those following them.

18 / THE PSYCHOLOGY (PERSONAL PAIN & MOTIVE)

Let's consider the psychological framework that develops in a person taught the way of idolatry and dependence on human leaders above and over God. In Israel's case, the people had followed **the sin cycle.** They'd fallen under the hands of pagan kings, only to be misled, disappointed, and then left frantically and desperately pleading for help. The Lord delivered them and brought rest, yet the psychological tailspin continued.

The real cycle, at its core, should read something like this; **I don't need God**, and then oops, wait … I was wrong … **I do need God.** When the people of Israel got comfortable in the gracious rest of God, they became complacent and forgetful. Fear set in. They gave in to the lie that they needed gods they could see. They needed assurance. They reached. They grabbed a new king, and uttered, "See, I don't need God, I just need a man." Phew. Problem solved.

And yet let's consider for a moment the psychological and mental problems that developed in the people when this process kept on going without a remedy or salvation. The following verses tell us exactly what we become when we buy into the belief that we don't need God, we only need ourselves. Consider 1 Samuel 8:10-22 for instance:

> So Samuel told all the words of the Lord to the people who were asking for a king from him. He said, "These will be the ways of the king who will reign over you: he will take your sons and appoint them to his chariots and to be his horsemen and to run before his chariots. And he will appoint for himself commanders of thousands and commanders of fifties, and some to plow his ground and to reap his harvest, and to make his implements of war and the equipment of his chariots. He will take your daughters to be perfumers and cooks and bakers. He will take the best of your fields and vineyards and olive orchards and give them to his servants. He will take the tenth of your grain and of your vineyards and give it to his officers and to his servants. He will take your male servants and female servants and the best of your young men and your donkeys, and put them to his work. He will take the tenth of your flocks, and you shall be his slaves. And in that day you will cry out because of your king, whom you have chosen for yourselves, but the Lord will not answer you in that day."
>
> But the people refused to obey the voice of Samuel. And they said, "No! But there shall be a king over us, that we also may be like all the nations, and that our king may judge us and go out before us and fight our battles." And when Samuel had heard all the words of the people, he repeated them in the ears of the Lord. And the Lord said to Samuel, "Obey their voice and make them a king."

Did you catch it? The people **listened** to Samuel describe the absolute inevitable mess that would come after the election of their so-called-king, and yet they never **heard** the warning. Samuel describes the destruction. He warns them of the third-degree-burn they will receive when they touch that burner, and yet curiosity still kills the cat. The Israelites still consider themselves a cat with more than nine lives, and they chant, "Give us a king, and give us death." This is the sad chant of bondage, not freedom. In saying, "We don't need God," they were welcoming into play all other taskmasters, and allowing them full control. Sin and death seek only to master. To control. To kill. To destroy. The psychology of "I don't need God," is a mindset fascinated with death. Even though God was clear in telling the people of their coming consequences, the people still cried, "Imprison us."

Notice also the Lord's response. He does not say "give" them a king, he says "**make** them a king." To give a king, the Lord must only give himself. Freedom. However, these people weren't looking for a king, they were looking for an idol. Something made. Make believe. Fairy tale. Placebo.

The psychology of humanity, when left on our own, is troubling because it continues toward problems, not solutions. Humanity wants made cures. Temporary, but not true. Our problem continues into today in the form of Rex Riddle-esque situations, the WWCG, and those that follow their lead. We fashion things, ourselves, or others into our image, and then we are enslaved by that image.

Don't hear me wrong. I'm not discounting Scripture's real emphasis placed upon the value of qualified overseers. Scripture is very clear on the importance of the character and heart of overseers. What I am getting at is what one of my professors in college would have called the formation of "cultic Christianity." My professor once pointed out the difference between occult and cult, and adequately made the point that many Christians are moving into a teaching model that enforces more "cultic ways of mandated thinking and training" over and above giving people a "paradigm that releases people to follow the Lord." We train people today in what to believe, not how to think. We make them dependent on us. We require that everyone dresses the same, talks the same, and looks the same. It's only then we can control things. This is what results when an idol sets up shop in our midst. We stop looking like Jesus, and we start trying to look like someone or something else.

Today, different denominations carry their own slogans, catchphrases, and "things you have to do to be part of us." The stipulations extend way beyond simple salvation and Baptism, and they begin fashioning communities that are more **uniform** and not **unified.** Unity is healthy. Uniformity is destructive. Whereas unity functions in the grey and allows a place for solidified truth to dwell in harmony with discovery, mystery, uncertainty, faith, questioning, differences of opinion, and growing into maturity, uniformity asks everyone to think in black and white. It tarnishes the truth. It subdues personality. It obliterates uniqueness. It gets rid of growth. It's false protection. When in a system of uniformity, we now are to "talk this way, not that way." Our struggles are minimized. Our uniqueness is demonized. On and on it goes.

What remains unaddressed in **uniformity** is the human heart. The behavior might appear to change or "conform" to what's expected, but the inside of a man/woman is never touched. We see this in both the case of Rex and Samuel. Though the leaders of Samuel's day tried everything in their power to move the people away or toward God, it was clear that as long as the people were dependent on a system that demanded a leader that was "altogether other than Jesus," they continued on in darkness. Once Samuel died, they had nothing truthfully real in their heart to lead them. Likewise, once Rex was taken overseas, the people turned outward for guidance and forgot that the Holy Spirit lives inside.

Nevertheless, there's hope. Another perspective remains. Transformation begins with the words, **"I do need God."**

19 / COMMUNITY PAIN & MOTIVE

Before we discuss needing God and the many amazing gospel remedies that can help us to heal in our Rex/Judge-ridden tendencies, let's say just a few things here about how our psychology impacts the formation of the community.

When insecure **people** are left to themselves under the wrongful idolatrous objects or people they cling to, they become an insecure **people.** Fearful. Insecure people resign and allow their leaders to do things for them. Insecure peoples consume and fail to produce. Insecure peoples are locked in fear, and so they can never be expected to step out in faith. Insecure peoples are dependent on their teachers like a baby suckling a mother's breast. They never move to a place of using a fork. They never chew. Too much effort.

Insecure peoples isolate. They guard their own. They self-protect. Isolated and insecure peoples grow selfish, and the community dwindles in true service and love. These so-called "communities" lose any sense of one another.

Sure, an overlord that demands people's obedience can still

persuade insecure peoples to erect an altar of false worship or do something that blatantly devalues their beliefs through acts of coerced service. Nevertheless, forced service is not service. It's mandated. It's slavery. The best we can hope for in a community that follows under sheer control is a **religion of duty**, not of **love.**

Where we all end up when we follow this way is ultimately a place where **"we are the authority."** We know what's best for us. Everyone else's thoughts are suspect. God's voice is suspect. We're independent. When God says don't touch the burner or you'll get hurt, we interpret that like a selfish two-year-old who thinks "I wonder what fun they are trying to hide?" Our opinion becomes supreme. We get loud. We get viral. We get on social media, and the world becomes full of voices that are self-inflated. Why? Because if I'm the authority, then you need to listen to me.

The best a king can be amongst a people clinging to their own authority is a celebrity. Israel wanted a handsome king. They wanted someone who would "fight their battles for them" (1 Sam. 8:20). They did not want to lift a finger at the cost of breaking a nail. They wanted a person who made them look good and attended to their every whim and fancy. The only purpose they longed for in a government at all was so that big government could go out and acquire all the resources of the world in an effort to fill the bellies of those back at home.

A bleak picture, eh? Quite. It's revealing. We can see ourselves in this progression. We can see our divided nations in this progression. We can see how all the hurts, slander, gossip, violence, tantrums, complaining, and the like, originate in this place in us that despises authority.

So when the Israelites say, "We want a king who will judge us …" let me interpret what this statement really means. The undercurrent says something more to this effect: We want a king who will flatter us, and tell us that in all things that we judge rightly.

We want our judgments affirmed. We want our ways mandated. We want our comforts prioritized. We want to be listened to, but not admonished. We want to be fed, but we never want to exert the effort required to feed. We want to be chiefs, not Indians, and if forced to be a tribe, we want a tribe that only looks like us.

There is a glorious remedy. It is found in needing God. The confession of a man, woman, or child that proclaims "We need God" exposes and brings to an end the deceptive power of all the WWCGs in our world. It brings the Babylonian system to its knees. It brings to an end the stressful burden that the Rex Riddles in our lives carry. It fills the work of Samuels with joy once again. It trains families to be free. Needing God is our only way out of fear. It's our only way to avoid control and yet still remain in control. Needing God is the only way to posture ourselves in love toward another; all while avoiding the logical end of selfishness in every form.

So what does needing God look like in remedy? How can we identify places in our leadership fallouts, structures, or methods that loudly scream the opposite of what we intend—namely that we do not need God? How can we die to our need as leaders to create in others a need for us, and how can we forgive those in our life that have made us too dependent on them? How can we heal from where we've made idols of others, only to be disappointed and left broken?

Let me share a few things that I feel have helped me, and will hopefully be equally as helpful to you—in your leadership and in your following.

1. Freedom came to me when I realized that the Bible is written in principles and paradigms, not mandates and methods. It has helped me lead people toward dependence on God, not me.

Paradigms use Principles in teaching us **how to think**. Mandates and Methods teach us **what to think.** If you learn how to think, you can learn anywhere you go with God as your teacher. If you learn what to think, you're dependent on whoever taught you to continue to force-feed you what they think. Whereas paradigms and principles supply us with a basic framework that can then be used freely in any situation, mandates and methods make us dependent on someone else's way of thinking.

For example, if you were to play basketball, as your coach, I would teach you a few paradigms. Dribble, Pass, Shoot. I would teach you the value of the team over the individual player. That's it. Once you embrace the paradigm, you can go play freely. The simplicity allows for a variety of methods, personalities, skills, positions, variables, and approaches to flourish, and yet no one person has to be in there like The Riddler mandating everyone's behavior. Therefore, a three-point shooter can best decide when to make that shot, and when to pass it into the forward who is more accustomed to hook shots, fade-aways, and layups. He's operating under a deeper paradigm. Team dictates the decision.

Each player in the game of basketball has to operate from the same set of basic principles—to play basketball you need to master dribbling, shooting, passing, and teamwork. Every other variable on the court is open to the person's skill and gifting, as long as it supports these things. When these things break down, so does the game.

Paradigms prioritize ways of being and thinking, and they are so much easier to learn. They are a posture we take in all things. Take for example Jesus' emphasis on **faith, hope, and love.** These are principles and paradigms. They are the dribble, pass, and shoot of the believer's life. Why is this helpful? Well, let's say you live a life of suffering, torment, rape, and the like, and I live a life of luxury, success, and ease. As the rich one, I may make you out to be awful because your method didn't work. You may hate me because my life is too easy when in reality both of us still have three paradigms that must control our life: **faith, hope, and love**. Neither of us can see the end of our life, and both of us are commanded to do the same thing by our God—to love God and love others, etc.

Paradigms teach a basic set of principles to live by. They allow us to be flexible in situations. They allow us to be human in situations. Principles stress ways of conduct, character, and being, over and above ways of doing and strict ways of thinking.

When we are handed things foreign to us, principles and paradigms help us to adjust and successfully manage new things with truthful actions. Our doing is changed more thoroughly as a result. Paradigms prioritize unity in diversity. Paradigms allow for the perspective of the other, as well as a way to hold the other accountable to essential truths. Paradigms allow for solid truth and principle to flesh out in and through a variety of personalities while still aiming at a common goal. Paradigms are colorfully together. Mandates and methods are vanilla and isolated.

Consider again my basketball analogy. What would happen if a game was driven more by mandate and method over paradigm? What would happen if a coach were to require one zone defensive style and only teach three plays? What would happen if this team was then to meet an opponent that requires more man-to-man defense, and requires more than three plays to win? What if the coach sees that his plan is not working and rather than adjust instead says, "Keep doing it this way." Well, number one, this is ineffective. Two, the players have only learned how to apply their skills in a handful of situations, but when anything truly difficult comes, they are ill-prepared. They are defeated. They are imprisoned. They are dependent on their coach to tell them what to do. They have no design for how to think themselves.

Now compare this to the model of modern-day preaching. Generally speaking, preachers today have become more pragmatic in preaching. They monologue, and rarely ever dialogue. They employ a "this is what I think" style of preaching over the priority of helping people think and interpret Scripture correctly for themselves. Compare this to the priority of question-asking that Jesus models in his teaching. **For every one statement Jesus makes in the gospels, he asks four questions**. This might be worth some good thought in learning how we might better disciple people to develop their own convictions over and above relying on ours.

For the modern preacher of today, the Bible becomes a manual for success. If we do certain things we'll acquire certain results. Our Bible lessons are three points. Our illustrations are bullet points. It's black and white. Teaching is a mandate and method, not a paradigm and principle. There's no room for questioning, variety, contradiction, or growth. It just "is what it is."

People either grow dependent on the preacher to feed them what he thinks and yet lack any skills to feed themselves, or they rebel while still lacking the tools to come to truth. Either a cultic situation of control will form, like with WWCG; an overly dependent situation will form, like with Rex, or an overt rebellion will form like in the days of Samuel. Because the individual has only been armed with what to believe and has never been taught to question it, internalize it, teach it, and understand it, they are left without tools and conviction.

I see the above all the time as a Pastor and Professor. People of all ages come to me sporting what their denomination thinks, their pastor thinks, or the latest greatest Christian personality thinks. They are utterly taken aback when I say, "What do you think?" More importantly, "How does what you think, or what they think compare to what Scripture actually says?" Almost immediately I get to their deep waters with my pointed questions. I get to what's in them. They begin to divulge to me the convictions they have embraced—what they've heard—and what they have chosen not to hear.

Once I begin to discover what is deepest in them, I don't tell them what I think,—though many will still attempt to pin me into a corner in desperation to know what I think—I will rather lead them in a process of **hermeneutics.** Basically, this fancy word means a "right way of teaching and learning to interpret." I will teach them how to learn the Bible's context and authorship, to internalize and process it for themselves, and I will show them how to find every passage's **one true intended meaning**. I will teach them how to feed themselves with the truth of God, not the error of their own thinking, and then I will ask them to compare what they think to what God thinks.

I will then ask, "Do you agree with God?" If their answer is no, I recognize they are a person who is still struggling with rebellion—and don't we all struggle in this regard? If they agree to what the Bible says, they are someone longing for obedience. In both cases, more questions are needed. We don't just write the person off if they disagree, we press them to prove why they disagree. If they say they agree, we have to examine their whole life and ask if God is still working to press out this truth into their whole life.

The redeeming element is that the gospel is about walking with our God in friendship. He's not a dictator. He's a friend. He walks through questions, complaints, doubts, four-letter words, anger, betrayal, heartache and everything in between. If people relate to God only as one who judges us, like the people of Israel, they really don't understand God. Imagine how much freedom a person is going to feel in expressing their doubts if they're in the presence of one who judges them? Not much! But if they feel they are in the presence of one who listens (Rex), and yet one who will also challenge their thinking with the truth of God (Samuel), growth will skyrocket. The gospel will transform the person.

2. Freedom came to me when I realized that the Bible speaks of disciples, overseers, character, and equippers over and above talking about leaders.

I'm utterly sick today at how many books are out on leadership, and not one book explores how to follow well. Why isn't there a book on the greatest learners? Our absence of solid teaching on trust and following doesn't make sense because Jesus recruited followers and called them disciples (which means learners). Yet all our titles in churches, work, and play, and the like, seem to point to our expertise, not our humility. What's formed is a mentality of people who are obsessed with leadership and its office.

Ironically, the only one in Scripture who is portrayed as a leader, a Visioner and a goal setter, as we would typically define a leader, is God. Jesus. Think back for a moment to the Israelites in the desert. God led them wherever he wished. When he stopped, they stopped by fire, and when he moved in the daytime via a cloud, the people moved. He knew where they were going. He knew their goal. He knew where their enemies were. All they did was follow.

The above facts are why I think that when leaders are spoken of in the New Testament, they are always referenced as leaders by their character. They are referred to by who they are, not what they do. In the gospel, Jesus prioritizes the man over the method. He prioritizes love over the gifting. He prioritizes the heart before the action.

Understanding leadership in the aforementioned way makes our leadership more about submitting and following Christ. It requires us to look less at the horizon of our vision, and look more at the one we're seeking to become like. This results in a role change. When leaders are referenced in the New Testament they are spoken more of as equippers and overseers, not leaders. By overseeing and equipping, they lead. They don't take people anywhere. God does. If a man tries to lead man, idolatry is the only thing that develops.

However, if leaders focus on equipping people to act on paradigm and principle, they will free them to be the "priesthood of the believer" at their home, work, and play. Hundreds of creative visions can then spring forth freely, and yet be unified. The overseer's job simply becomes that of protecting the individual, watching for error, and encouraging and continuing to remind them of all God has said.

Why does this matter? It changes everything. It changes our church from consumers into producers. It welcomes even the craziest idea, and it shapes it with the gospel. Diversity happens. All races and creeds come together and rejoice in how different they are. Theology becomes more colorful. Theology creates embracing rather than division. All of us are challenged to change and grow. We're not waiting for orders from man, but we are obeying our free and vibrant God. This unleashes community in multiplication, not addition, and it takes the weight and exception off of leaders to make things happen.

3. Freedom came to me when I realized that leadership is measured in following, not in leading.

This may sound redundant from what I just got done explaining, but I want to say it again. Consider 1 Peter 2:21-25:

> **For to this you have been called**, because Christ also suffered for you, leaving you an example, so that you might follow in his steps. He committed no sin, neither was deceit found in his mouth. When he was reviled, he did not revile in return; when he suffered, he did not threaten, but continued entrusting himself to him who judges justly. He himself bore our sins in his body on the tree, that we might die to sin and live to righteousness. By his wounds you have been healed. For you were straying like sheep, but have now returned to the Shepherd and Overseer of your souls.

Notice how Jesus is defined by his trust in his Father. He's not leading. He's following. He's submitting. True power is found in one that can show all power and restrain all power, and here we see both. God, in Jesus, was holding back all wrath and anger and was extending all love and forgiveness at the same time. I wonder how a robust view of trusting submission might change our view of what actually leads.

Finally, consider the name that Jesus is given in this event; "the Overseer of our souls." The only time that Jesus is named as an Overseer in Scripture is in a moment where he's fully surrendered. He's putting forth no vision. He's outlining no game plan. There are no apparent goals. The only thing remaining is a simple man sprawled out before the Father in complete surrender—even to the point of death.

4. Freedom came to me when I realized that I'm at the mercy of my own heart, not the actions of others.

I lived in fear much of my life. I was always scared of how

other's actions and beliefs would impact me; in large part, because I perceived my Christian upbringing to be so restrictive. Because I grew up in a home that held to a model of Christianity that was so focused on **duty** over **love**, I grew to hate the whole thing because it robbed me of relationship with my parents and it felt confining.

I carried this wound into churches for many years. I carried this fear into government and world affairs. I carried this into my marriage and into the parenting of my own children until one day I was released by the realization that no one has control over me except my God. I can walk into a room full of drunks, heroin addicts, prostitutes, and false teachers, and the only power that people, pleasure, or substance have over me, is what my own heart will allow. There's no such thing as peer pressure in the sense that anyone can make us do anything that we don't agree to. There's only me-pressure.

When I realized the power of the Holy Spirit's governance, I can't say that I was healed, because I still deeply struggle with all this to some degree in a variety of areas, but I can say that I know where the remedy is. The gracious Holy Spirit now resides in this once violent man. The love of God now dwells in me; a man once a gossip and a slanderer. The living one lives in me; me, once the hater of souls.

This is an altogether different gospel than big church, denomination, big government, or top-tier structures of any kind. It's the opposite. Our God works from the ground up. He comes to earth so that we can go to heaven. Our God knows that nothing hanging over our head can ever be counted as a trustworthy authority, so what did our God do? He smeared his blood over the doorposts of our hearts. He lives in us. He lives with us. He works his will and authority out through us. God transforms us from within. He doesn't try to conform us from the outside.

Only an idiot would try and shove a weed back in its seed.

Everyone knows that a weed opens up from the inside of a seed. Same with a flower. Same with people. Our paradigms need to aim at the hearts of people so that they open, like we all do, from the inside out.

5. Freedom came to me when I realized that growth and conviction forms in questioning and listening, and in rebuke and admonishment.

I've been forever changed by how Jesus brings the gospel to us. He comes with parables and says ponder. He comes with questions and reveals our inner motives. He comes in the form of man, and says "Behold." He tells us to speak his word, and he says "Hear." He tells us "Look at creation," and along with it and through it we see his mind and his nature. Notice how all of the wars that we fight in order to come to the truth take effect **from the inside.** Jesus didn't give us twelve steps to success and say "Go do them." He taught in ways that were artful. He painted things that take consideration. He taught in ways that operated on our souls. He asked questions that forced us to give honest answers. He rarely even gave the answers. Then, and only then, did he preach.

I think we need to ponder the gospel more thoroughly in how we bring it to people. It comes in listening, processing, pondering, meditating, and questioning, but once the heart of the WWCG person or the "Israelite" is revealed, we must teach, rebuke, admonish, and train.

We must notice the order in which Scripture places the cart and the horse. Questions and inquiry first, training and correction as we go. I fear our seminaries and churches have been training very heavily on how to give people answers instead of giving paradigms that help us provoke the right questions. I think our books are focusing far too much on leading us and far too little on teaching us the joy of following. I fear we are assaulting the lost person far too often with a monologue and missing that all of Scripture is framed around the meal—an environment of dialogue. I'm concerned that our hardened street corners, pulpits, church warehouses, and stages actually undermine the gospel's imagery of family, household, sons, daughters, fathers, mothers, and the like.

When we really consider how the truth of this chapter changes us, we have to drill down to the deepest reason we do things. We have to ask ourselves, are we using methods or paradigms? Are we mandating people in slavery or are we freeing people through principle? Are we forming chiefs or Indians? Are we forming humble followers or arrogant leaders? Are we shaping our environments and methods to press out and away from us, or are they like a boomerang, where everything always returns back into our hands?

The remedy for all of us that struggle toward WWCG-tendencies—over control, Rex-tendencies—pastoral enabling, or Israelite-tendencies—desiring someone or something else more than God, is not as simple as saying *I forgive*. We desperately need new systems, new ways of doing life, and to rediscover some of our roots and less-sexy ways of doing church. In that, we may just find that a different kind of community forms. That's the best medicine. That's the best protection. That's the best for all of us.

21 / QUESTIONS FOR DISCUSSION

First, contemplate these questions individually and answer in the space provided, and then join together collectively as a group. Here are some Scriptures that can help guide your discussion:

Verses to Consider: *Ti. 3:1-11; 1 Tim. 4:2-5; Mt. 10; 1 Cor. 2:9-16; Col. 2:8-15.*

1. How have you seen false teaching enter the family and church in our world today? In what areas are you prone to believe false teaching?

2. How can we play a positive role, similar to Rex Riddle, in being a good listener to others as they process truth?

. . .

3. In what ways can we seek to right the faults of Rex Riddle, and stand up to people's unbiblical ways of understanding God's Word, Jesus, and the world in which we live?

4. Do you tend to struggle with being too passive or aggressive toward others with the wrong understanding of truth? What sins in your life influence you in either direction?

5. Why do you think we as humans have such a desire for a human king, denomination, or visual system to lead us and feed us? On the contrary, why do you think people believe it to be correct to function without any sense of authority or responsibility?

6. How has the church and typical family approaches today actually shaped us for dependence and consumption of resources, over and above equipping us for service and producing (the mandate given to Adam)?

7. As suggested in the remedy portion of this chapter, how are we measuring success in our culture today by people who lead better, rather than by people who follow better?

8. How does following the Lord make us into natural leaders? How can we better equip those in our lives to follow Jesus, not just learn about him?

. . .

9. How can we help ourselves and those under our care and connect the ministry of the Holy Spirit and his leading to his role in bringing us back to the nature of Jesus as revealed in Scripture?

PART 4
GIVE UP OR GIVE OUT

22 / THE CASE STUDY

A man of integrity. That is how most people know Simre. He says the right thing, he does the right thing; it seems he's always ready to do exactly what is needed in every situation. His reputation is unmatched. Once a leader of an international church-planting organization, and a planter of many churches himself, Simre is now the Pastor of a little church of about 100 people in the city of Calcutta, India.

Simre's loyal followers will tell you that one of his strengths is finance. Simre has a long history of fiscal honesty and quite the resume of those he's exposed and brought to justice in their corruption in his little corner of Calcutta. His history with money, management skills, and pastoral flavor, attracts accountants, business professionals, and many people in similar industries who think Simre is nothing but a breath of fresh air. He invites generous giving through God's people toward causes that are helpful for the community of Calcutta, and people trust him.

Simre has been married to Aya for going on twenty-five years. Their marriage is comfortable and familiar. Simre views his wife much in the same manner as money. She's a commodity. He invests her life wherever possible in the work of the church, and yet unlike money, he reaps very little reward. Aya grows more resentful, distant, and out of love with Simre each and every day.

Benm, Sumaj, and Aisha are Simre's three children. Sumaj, the oldest, is off to college in The States soon enough, Aisha is the local trouble child, and Benm is the local soccer hero. Benm is certainly Simre's favorite. Simre's parents died early in his life, leaving him a homeless beggar, and he had always dreamed of being a soccer star. Simre lives out his dream through Benm.

One could say that Simre's family holds up under a great deal of responsibility. It may be better to say that they fall apart secretly under great pressure.

One day, the pressure became too much.

In the year 1999, Simre hit reality. Traveling intensely as a church planter and Pastor extraordinaire left Simre and his family in burn out. Their marriage, body, spirit, and children, buckle under the pressure. Aya disconnects. She vacates her ministry position, and the only time anyone sees anything of her is at the local fitness studio where she works out. She is done being a commodity.

Simre crashes. Physically he collapses via adrenaline burnout from years of ignoring his body. All the years of pushing through the stress leave him physically in a state of forever fatigue. He sleeps constantly. He shows up for work occasionally, and from the pulpit he is a manic mess. He breaks down emotionally during every sermon, he is belligerent toward the staff behind closed doors, and his kids fall to pieces.

Sumaj performs. He pretends he's okay and yet his drug of choice is pleasure. He dates a girl from the wrong side of the tracks in an effort only to have an escape. Meanwhile he lives underneath the shadow of his younger brother Benm. The star. Because Benm is so much better and well-loved than he is, Sumaj embraces the lie that he's worthless, and he fills each day with envy, jealousy, competition, and hostility. Aisha only increases in her rebellion. She never tried to pretend. She brings her mess to church. She shows up high and drunk and parades around with an endless barrage of boyfriends for the whole church to see. Benm implodes in shame and falters under the weight of Simre's expectations for him. Simre continues to outlet all his hopes and pressures on Benm, and Benm collapses.

Simre does everything he can to make Benm perfect at sports in hopes that one of his children might shine in the darkness while everything else falls apart. Benm keeps up the show, but barely, and is humiliated inside. His Dad is the loudest one on the bench. The coaches know that Simre stinks of control, and everyone within a hundred feet of Benm starts to recognize the stench. Benm is alone.

Trouble is, the elders at the church seem oblivious. The church either overlooks the trouble or lives in ignorance. Bottom line, people at the church remain so loyal to Simre that they actually embrace his burnout in a manner that convinces Simre that he's growing more pastoral and in touch with his emotions. The staff, on the other hand, knows better. They catch the tough end of everything. Simre shows up to meetings late, lifts his legs onto the table like a teenager, surfs social media, and only lends his opinion when he wants to show off the fact that his anger is as immature as his muscle shirt.

Simre is in full blown burnout. Some call it a midlife crisis. Some say it's the result of how hard he works. Some say it's because he carries a lot on his shoulders. I prefer to name his struggle what it is, pride. Sin.

Simre spent his whole life fighting out of gutters to survive, and this time wasn't going to be any different. Grace is not a concept that works for him. Grit and grind are things he relates to. As he has many times before, he attempts to pull himself up by his own boot straps, ride on his talents, all while attempting to convince others he's okay. But this time, it doesn't work. He can't hide behind personality this time. The sermons get more works based. The gospel of grace disappears, and around every turn, Simre seems to be faced with a choice: surrender to grace, or never give in. He chooses the latter. He keeps fighting.

The church follows suit. They follow his leadership into the pit of joyous works. Faith is lost, grace becomes a cuss word, and the gospel is lost in the wake of self-effort, cloaked integrity, 12-steps to success teaching, and veiled attempts to call strife living faith.

23 / THE STORY

et's share a similar story from Scripture that may help us work through the scenario with Simre.

PHARAOH KNOWS the Israelites are growing in number. Too many. Something has to be done in order to ensure that the Israelites do not become strong enough to overtake his kingdom. He commands that all the Hebrew boys be killed.

His order of murder spreads through the land. Israelite boys in the land of Egypt are killed in every household. Screams sound. Grief overwhelms. Suddenly a little basket comes drifting down the river into the hands of Pharoah's daughter. As she peels back the lid, her heart fills with compassion. She knows this little one is one of the boys ordered to be killed. She lifts the three-month baby from the river raft, finds him a wet nurse to feed him, and without even knowing it she places the baby back into the arms of his sister and mother for care-taking.

The child grows older, and his birth mother takes him to Pharoah's daughter to raise him in the palace. His name …

Moses. Moses flourishes in the palace. He's educated. He's fed. He's promoted. He leads slave owners and becomes just like the Egyptians.

But one day, the tides shift. Moses witnesses a violent beating in the street. An Egyptian hurting an Israelite. Moses lifts his hand. He strikes. He kills the Egyptian. He buries him. Moses flees to Midian to hide. Moses meets his wife Zipporah and works as a Shepherd in the desert amongst his father-in-law Jethro's flocks. One day, however, God interrupts Moses' plans to remain in hiding. God sees his people's sufferings, and he elects Moses to be their deliverer. God commands Moses to go back to Egypt.

With much hesitation, Moses obeys. Through Moses God brings ten devastating plagues of wrath against the ten "gods" of the Egyptians. He ruins the Egyptians for ruining his people. The last plague brings death to Pharoah's son, and Pharaoh finally agrees to free God's people from slavery in an effort to stop God from bringing more destruction. The Israelites flee. They wander toward the land that God plans to give them as they follow God in fire by night and in a cloud by day.

After God delivers the Israelites again from the Egyptians in the famous parting of the Red Sea, Moses settles the people next to what is known as the "mountain of God" near Midian. Hearing that Moses had again returned into the desert, Jethro, Moses' father-in-law, travels to meet Moses and brings along with him Zipporah and Moses' two boys.

Jethro runs to Moses in an embrace. We get a glimpse into the reuniting of this family in Exodus 18:

> Then Moses told his father-in-law all that the Lord had done to Pharaoh and to the Egyptians for Israel's sake, all the hardship that had come upon them in the way, and how the Lord had delivered them. And Jethro rejoiced for all the good that the

Lord had done to Israel, in that he had delivered them out of the hand of the Egyptians.

Jethro said, "Blessed be the Lord, who has delivered you out of the hand of the Egyptians and out of the hand of Pharaoh and has delivered the people from under the hand of the Egyptians. Now I know that the Lord is greater than all gods because in this affair they dealt arrogantly with the people." And Jethro, Moses' father-in-law, brought a burnt offering and sacrifices to God; and Aaron came with all the elders of Israel to eat bread with Moses' father-in-law before God.

Jethro rejoices in Moses' return. Zipporah is with her husband again. The two boys are with their Father again. It's a wonderful scene of celebration. But more is happening than just a celebration.

Moses is in need of attention. The work and the demand for the deliverance in Egypt leaves him weary. Though the Israelites are free, they fail to act like it. Moses leads more than two million people toward God's promises while all they do is gripe and complain. Moses is tired. Jethro sees the fatigue in Moses firsthand the following day. This is how Exodus 13:18-26 records the event:

> The next day Moses sat to judge the people, and the people stood around Moses from morning till evening. When Moses' father-in-law saw all that he was doing for the people, he said, "What is this that you are doing for the people? Why do you sit alone, and all the people stand around you from morning till evening?"
>
> And Moses said to his father-in-law, "Because the people come to me to inquire of God; when they have a dispute, they come to me and I decide between one person and another, and I make them know the statutes of God and his laws."

Moses' father-in-law said to him, "What you are doing is not good. You and the people with you will certainly wear yourselves out, for the thing is too heavy for you. You are not able to do it alone. Now obey my voice; I will give you advice, and God be with you! You shall represent the people before God and bring their cases to God, and you shall warn them about the statutes and the laws, and make them know the way in which they must walk and what they must do. Moreover, look for able men from all the people, men who fear God, who are trustworthy and hate a bribe, and place such men over the people as chiefs of thousands, of hundreds, of fifties, and of tens. And let them judge the people at all times. Every great matter they shall bring to you, but any small matter they shall decide themselves. So it will be easier for you, and they will bear the burden with you. If you do this, God will direct you, you will be able to endure, and all this people also will go to their place in peace."

Fatigue, burnout, and exhaustion make any human do things they might not ordinarily do. We may be able to boil the above scenario down to Moses' immaturity and growing management skills, or maybe even say, "Jethro is just extremely wise." Regardless of what our conclusion, I think some of the choices that Moses makes result from a man who has grown too tired. In Egypt, he'd been the messenger to carry God's wrath out upon Egypt, while at the same time being used of God to bring deliverance to Israel. He is "the guy." Everyone looks to him. **He accepts the pressure but doesn't quite consider the toll it will take.**

24 / THE PSYCHOLOGY (PERSONAL PAIN & MOTIVE)

The common thread that links the story of Simre together with the biblical scenario of Moses might be summarized this way: "when doing the work of God, it's easy to take that work upon yourself." In both instances we can see what taking too much ownership in gospel work can do. In Simre's case, he burned out. In Moses' case, he was about to burn out.

What leads anyone to burn out?

Expectations. Missed expectations. Simre carried around a silent expectation of himself and God. His subtle sin was believing that his main role was to **be the Savior**, not point to the Savior. Everyone depended on him. Everyone looked to him. People expected Simre to carry burdens with a smile. They expected him to almost be perfect. It is perfect that killed him. It is perfect that destroyed the health of his family.

Moses was well on his way to buying into the same lie, and why not? It seems easy, doesn't it? God used Moses in a mighty way. Moses felt responsible for the Israelites. He felt guilt over the man he'd murdered. He felt shame in running away, but let's be honest, he also felt powerful to some degree in coming back.

Though the story of Exodus clearly shows Moses being real with his weaknesses, it also clearly portrays Moses as one daringly foolish enough to sit down before two-million people as a judge. Maybe he overestimated what God wanted him to do. Maybe he let a little pride set in. Either way, Jethro helped Moses realize that **the work of God** is one that is **shared.** It's a together work. God's yoke is easy and his burden is light. Only our missed expectations and our possible over-prioritization of our place in the mix is what causes burnout.

We may find ourselves thinking, "Well, it is not so bad. At least Simre and Moses are wasting themselves on good work." True. However, when we step into God's place as Judge, and the Savior of his people, we might **commit** only small visible sins, but our **omission** causes far greater injustices to surface.

Moses' small sin may have been to grow a tiny bit nearsighted in his fatigue, but a bigger sin loomed on the horizon. When a person carries an out-of-proportion load in one area of life, it leaves less strength to hold things together in the other hand. Moses omitted his greater responsibility to his family and to sound governance of God's people. Jethro had to step in and help Moses to see the long term effects if he continued on in his less-than-thoughtful plan.

Consider Zipporah. We originally know that Zipporah left to go to Egypt with Moses (Ex. 4:18-20), but not too long after in Exodus 18 we are told that Jethro brings the family back to Moses. We are never really told when or why Zipporah is sent back home while Moses continues to Egypt, but Exodus 4 lends us some clues. In the midst of their journey to Egypt, Moses fell ill. God struck him with illness for failing to circumcise his son. Being too sick to do it himself, Zipporah performs the procedure. Zipporah and the Midianite people abhorred the ritual, and in Exodus 4:25 she says to Moses: "Surely you are a husband of blood to me."

Zipporah's statement exhibits her hurt. We might speculate that Moses sent Zipporah home because she was mad at him, and he could not deal with the conflict at the moment. He may have sent her away because the family was distracting him from the mission. We may even say that his actions were noble, and he sent her away to protect her and his newborn son from what was about to happen in Egypt. One thing we can say for sure is that Moses had neglected in part his role at home. God had commanded him to circumcise his son, and Moses did not do it. Perhaps he was too busy. He had other things on his mind. Egypt was more important. Whatever the excuse we can possibly invent, Moses was human, like Simre.

Simre's neglect and objectifying overuse of his family are much clearer to us, but they are nevertheless the same. In the world's eyes, we might say Simre **committed** a small sin in neglecting his family while doing *good things*. We might say the same about Moses, but look what their active sins caused them to **passively omit.** Family. The damage done particularly in the case of Simre, shows us how deep a passive sin can run.

His wife burned out. His son, Benm crumbled under the weight of his father's expectations. Benm became Simre's idol of choice. Sumaj was altogether overlooked and underloved, and Aisha was obviously reaching out for attention.

Often times, it's the loves we negligently fail to give that hurt more than the sins we actively perform. Putting mission over family is one sin that is subtle and passive, but it causes active hurt.

Both Simre and Moses chose not to fulfill their role and responsibility to those in their home. This neglect led Simre to full-fledged burnout. He not only failed to attend to his home, but also to his own health. In Moses' case, we must thank God for Jethro. Moses was definitely headed down the same road as Simre had not Jethro intervened with amazing wisdom. Jethro's timely advice helped Moses avoid a landmine. If Moses would have attempted to bear the burdens of the two million people under his care (God's job), his burn out would have been one thousand times worse than Simre's.

Positively, and it's good to mention one positive, Moses listened. He heeded Jethro's advice. Simre, on the other hand, spent years ignoring people's warnings. Many had sought to counsel him in a variety of areas in his life, and pride kept him from listening.

Simre and Moses were both left with the same two choices and they responded differently: **give up or give out.**

Giving up. Surrender. Humility. Rest. These are words we normally associate with cowards. However, when one gives up to God and surrenders to a greater power, humility becomes power. In surrender we find grace. Grace is found when we set down our pocket knife in an all-out knife fight in order to allow the God of heaven to step in with a meat cleaver. By surrendering to a greater power we become stronger.

Moses became stronger in his thinking even while struggling with sin.

Simre grew weaker. He chose not to give up, but to give out. He was a fighter on the streets. He had to fight to survive. He didn't need help. He didn't need grace. His rusty pocket knife was just fine. You can keep your meat cleaver. Inevitably Simre's fight gave out. His weapon couldn't match up even as Simre lay there on the ground, bloody and dying, still chanting, "I can still get up. I can still do this."

Simre sang this song to the death of his body. Simre chanted this to the detriment of the family. Simre preached twelve steps to success to psych himself up toward doing it himself, and once again, it burned him out.

Did you catch the psychology of sin in both scenarios? Sin says, "I can do anything," and yet sin takes everything. The grace of our good God in heaven says, "I can do everything, and yet I take nothing. I give!"

Sin is a thief. It steals. It kills. It destroys. It makes us into destroyers. It makes us into thieves. It makes us into killers and takers, not givers.

25 / COMMUNITY PAIN & MOTIVE

What do you think the mentality of **taking** does to a community? What do you think the psychology of **"I can do this myself"** does to a community?

It collapses leaders, for one. It rips health out of the picture, and for those already hurting, it leaves no one around filled with the power of God to help people bear the slack of their own sufferings.

It collapses the lung and life-breath of a community. The people learn to wear out their family and omit their responsibility to build up the home. The people learn the independence of "I" and "me," not "we" and "us." The community loses fathers. The kids lose parents. The mothers struggle along as widows that are married. Compromise enters. Roles are confused. God is ignored. The physical body gets sick and the Body of Christ limps. The result? A home that's malnourished results in a people that are starving.

We might now have an idea as to why the Benm's of the world collapse in shame, depression, suicide, and the like. We might understand why Sumaj's waste themselves in drink, fleeting pleasures, and broken highs. We might even now understand why the Aisha's run into the arms of those that only seek abuse while calling it love.

Simre-types fashion communities that have a taste for junk food. The communal body craves health, yet they reach for junk. They crave nutrition and sustenance and run to donuts. Their body craves real pleasure, and yet runs away from the Lord to get it.

All in all, God's efforts are replaced by mankind's. The community loses all trust in God's ability to provide. They only trust their ability to go out and "get." All faith and rest are lost to the god of striving, pulling ourselves up by our own bootstraps, and effort. The God of Rest no longer makes sense.

And when people act out of fatigue and not rest, all is lost. Fatigue clouds the mind. It makes wisdom impossible. It does not choose hard things. Burden chokes out life. It chokes out creativity. It ends beauty. Everything becomes functional. Utility. Money. Data. Hard.

Rest is the remedy. I'm not talking in terms of naps and eight hours of shut-eye. Though this is important. I'm speaking of rest in terms of the gospel. I'm speaking of a Savior who says, "Come unto me all you who are weary and of heavy burden and I will give you rest. My yoke is easy and my burden is light" (Mt. 11:28). I'm speaking of Jesus who refers to salvation in Hebrews as "entering his rest."

Rest is reality. It's realizing that all work has been done. The cross of Christ completed all work. It's finished. Finito. Done. Not in part, but complete. When a person rests in the fact that all vision has been signed, sealed, and delivered, that all goals have been checked, and that all dreams and aspirations have been fulfilled in the man of Jesus, a new posture sets in.

It's not that we stop working. Absolutely not. We work harder. We work **from** rest, not **for** rest. We work **from** love, not **for** love. We work **from** completion, not **for** completion. We work **from** victory not **for** victory. We lay back just a little bit, and we are able to give less to the advancing, and more to the moments. The people in our moments are most important. Our family. Our kids. Our homes. Our tables. *Where we are going becomes less* *important than the type of people we are becoming.* No longer are we burned out, stressed out, worried, anxious, suicidal, burdened, along with the slew of other psychological, medical, spiritual, social, and emotional symptoms that follow. No longer do we just accept burdens that we know will kill us, like Moses.

When we accept the remedy of rest—Jesus' rest, we can hear the Jethros more clearly. The Jethros of this world know that a lot of restless people have gotten the way they are out of good intention. It's a very subtle sin. Jethros don't judge, they counsel.

The Bible also counsels. It instructs. It Pastors. It Shepherds. Into the tired flocks of Simre the Bible says "Surrender." Surrender to God. Let him work. In Moses' case, he says surrender to others and trust them to work alongside you.

We talked earlier in this book regarding how the Bible teaches about "plural leadership." The situation with Moses teaches us about plural leadership. Why? Because it's the gospel. The Trinity. Leading as a unified one—together—is what it means to be Christlike. Becoming like Jesus is learning to be amongst the Father and the Holy Spirit. It's a together work. It's a we thing, not a me thing. God leads amongst friends, and so should people. It's healthy for us, and it's healthy for those that follow. It builds trust in those that lead, as we link arms and depend on the gifts of others, and it strengthens the sense of safety in the flock as they follow not one person, but many ***unified as one.***

In closing, I assume that many reading this see a bit of themselves, their situations, their churches, or their leaders in the scenarios I've mentioned. Maybe you're in the thick of exhaustion like Simre, or maybe you are young, proud, zealous, and lacking wisdom, and the way you are living your life is setting you up to burn out later on, as in the case of Moses. I would give this one last piece of advice in order to connect the dots of all that's been said thus far. To avoid Simre's fate, don't just scale back and do less. Your healing is found in prioritizing what God prioritizes. He values rest. He values the home. Restoration is found when the heart turns back to the children, not away from them. Redemption happens when parents think more about the home and less about work, not vice versa.

The remedy is not just a "fix it." It's not just to disappear into a nap. The remedy is a paradigm shift. It's the way a Christian lives. It's a posture toward all things. The center of all of Scripture is a meal, and home, and marriage. Toward this center, our way of life should point. It's the best way to recover. It's the best way to serve healthily. It's the best way to rest. It's the best way to become. It's the best way to lead. It is the kingdom of God.

27 / QUESTIONS FOR DISCUSSION

First, contemplate these questions individually and answer in the space provided, and then join together collectively as a group. Here are some Scriptures that can help guide your discussion:

Verses to Consider: *Eph. 4:8-10; Heb. 4:1-13; Lk. 1:13-17; Phil. 2:5-11.*

1. What signs in your own life point to whether or not you're working **for** love or **from** love? What's the difference?

2. How are we supposed to understand rest, peace, or "Shalom" as the Jews would call it, in a holistic and biblical way?

3. How can living in light of the finished work of Christ protect us from the typical over-achievement driven and stressful merry-go-round of the world?

. . .

4. Why is it so easy for us, like Simre, to turn our hearts toward work and ministry efforts, whereas the Scripture seems to imply that a Godly person is one whose heart is turned toward their children? Where's the balance?

5. How has our culture succeeded in tearing down the central fabric and value placed upon the closeness of family?

6. How can you put in place structures of humility and safety in your life now to ensure that you become like Moses when confronted by Jethro, rather than Simre when confronted by those surrounding him?

7. What idol lies at the root of us needing to do everything ourselves rather than following God's method of depending on his Body to do it with and for us?

8. Why is the Bible's structure of governance a plural model of leadership, rather than in a singular model of a Senior or CEO-type leadership?

9. Why is modeling our structure of leadership after the Triune God safe, freeing, and healthier than inventing our own view of organization?

PART 5
JUST A LITTLE BIT TO THE LEFT

"You'll pray and worship God more in ten weeks in our school than you have in your whole life in the church." I'll forever remember these words.

Asher is passionate. He's persuasive. He's convincing. He's intoxicating and perhaps overwhelming. He's different than a Pastor, he's a salesman.

Asher speaks to people's wounds. He convinces the weak they are no longer weak via his confidence and unquestioned strength. He flatters and calls it prophecy. He boasts about the future as if he's seen it. He stirs hope. He awakens those who call themselves failures. He rouses the "not good enough." He speaks to missed expectations. He sells a product, and it's not vacuums, but it's a promise of a supposed "wholehearted pursuit of God."

He speaks in judgment and criticism toward God's people, and yet claims to be the strongest of those that believe. He boasts "the real Christian life." He calls Christians "too worldly." and prides himself on how he beats his body into submission like Paul and values nothing but spiritual things. He speaks of anything in God's creation as lesser than, and says that it only leads to hurt. He's vocal as one who knows the hurt often caused by those in the local church. He identifies. He preys on people's bitterness. He heralds the language of one who is not content. He preaches rescue. He promises everyone that God will give them all they are hoping for.

Asher is the hype-man, but Shekinah boasts the power. She's the sidekick, but she's also the real show. She is full of divination and calls it the Holy Spirit. She teaches teleportation, reading minds, energy healings, and sells prayer cloths that contain her anointing. She teaches that Jesus is our servant and that we hold the keys to the kingdom, yet she twists both truths. Tearing what's real apart in wrong and heretical ways, she prays to Jesus not out of a spirit of request but in a posture of command.

For Shekinah, all the supernatural experiences in Scripture are prescriptive (rules and methods), not descriptive (occurrences perfectly timed to demonstrate specific purposes). The book of Acts, for example, is no longer a historical narrative, but a book of methods and practices for the church. Therefore, all that is in the Bible only serves to show us what we have the rights to as Christians. We, in turn, can make the sun stand still, heal whenever we choose, make the rain stop on a whim, cast literal mountains into the sea, raise the dead whenever we wish, and wield the hand of God's sovereignty in whichever direction might best serve our purpose.

Brett and Jade buy it all. They are young. All of sixteen. They are blind followers. With no background or training in how to rightly handle the Word of God, Brett and Jade buy into the nonsense. They fall into the ruse of wanting "all" of God.

Though the Bible is never opened when Asher or Shekinah are teaching, Brett and Jade claim to be Bible-believing Christians; yet they treat the Scriptures as old news. God's Word is spoken of as dead letters on the page. Mere words cannot equal experience, right? The Scriptures are used to provide a document of the ecstatic reality of our history's past. The Bible becomes a magic book and a wand. In the teachings of Asher and Shekinah, the Bible is never to be seen as the glorious revealing of our God made flesh—Jesus—the "perfect and exact representation of God's nature" (Heb. 1:3). The Bible is simply a starting place to begin our journey of becoming gods ourselves.

I n the Apostle Paul's ministry to Colossae, he encountered a phenomenon similar to that of Asher and Shekinah. Truth be told, the wildly rampant misinterpretation of the Biblical word "charismata"—where we get the name *charismatics*—is not a new thing. Rampant misuse and misunderstanding regarding the nature of God's beautiful spiritual ministries within his church have caused many divisions throughout history. Much of our learning or teaching on this subject has not been helpful. Unfortunately, as we'll see in the following case of the Gnostics, and in the case of those in Asher's school, the beliefs in many hyper-charismatic circles today (as opposed to a healthy understanding of what charismatic means) are closer to divination and a spirit-filled witchcraft, than actual Holy-Spirit-filled ministry.

One of the belief systems that pervaded the life and story of Paul is that of the Gnostics. We can safely assume that the epistle to the Colossians is dated to the period of 58-60 CE. It is commonly thought to have been written by Paul while he was imprisoned at Rome. Much of the Epistle directly rebukes the Gnostics.

Gnosticism and all remnants of it today are not a religion. Rather it's a philosophy that is blended with components of existing religions. Gnosticism in its basic claim asserts that salvation can be achieved through secret knowledge. Gnosticism becomes less about **who** you know and more about **what** you know. In this manner, knowledge is superior to faith and even truth. Those who are more enlightened look down on those with everyday knowledge and simply sigh in pity; "I'm so sorry they have not been given the secret."

At the core of this mysterious knowledge is the belief that matter (stuff) is bad, and spirit is good. Any god who might be reckoned as good cannot intermingle with his creation at all. Intertwining would pollute such a perfect deity. Gnostics reject the deity and humanity of Christ with the acclamation: "That's stupidity. How could a God, claiming to be holy, mix with us?"

A Gnostic might readily reject that prayer of Jesus that sounds something like this: "I pray Father **not** that you take them out of the world but that you **protect** them from the evil one." In his prayer, Jesus affirms that our spiritual presence in the physical world is an absolute necessity that can't be separated. Nonetheless, it's absolute craziness for a Gnostic to think of having a positive or redemptive posture within the world. The whole goal of spirituality to the Gnostic is to commune up to god. To leave. To get away. To be spiritually perfect has nothing to do with a body of any kind. We are encouraged to escape into something altogether beyond.

Believing in this way allowed for the Gnostics to indulge their flesh in many ways. They became sexually perverse in all matters imaginable because in their view any destructive treatment of the flesh has really no point at all. It's moot. It's void. The body is already something of rubbish.

Like Brett and Jade, the members of Colossi were buying into a gospel resembling a flavor of Gnosticism. In Colossians 1:9-12 Paul writes:

> For this reason we also, since the day we heard it, do not cease to pray for you, and to ask that you may be filled with the knowledge *[epignosin]* of His will in all wisdom and spiritual understanding; that you may walk worthy of the Lord, fully pleasing Him, being fruitful in every good work and increasing in the knowledge *[epignosin]* of God; strengthened with all might, according to His glorious power, for all patience and long-suffering with joy; giving thanks to the Father who has qualified us to be partakers of the inheritance of the saints in the light.

Paul emphasizes his desire that **all** might come to a knowledge of Christ's will. Paul's gospel is available to all, it's not a **secret.** Paul also clearly explains how a fullness of knowledge can only be found in the person of Christ (Col. 1:15-21):

> He is the image of the invisible God, the firstborn of all creation. For by him all things were created, in heaven and on earth, visible and invisible, whether thrones or dominions or rulers or authorities —all things were created through him and for him. And he is before all things, and in him all things hold together. And he is the head of the body, the church. He is the beginning, the firstborn from the dead, that in everything he might be preeminent. For in him all the fullness of God was pleased to dwell, and through him to reconcile to himself all things, whether on earth or in heaven, making peace by the blood of his cross. And you, who once were alienated and hostile in mind, doing evil deeds, he has now reconciled in his body of flesh by his death, in order to present you holy and blameless and above reproach before him ...

Paul attacks the Gnostic belief that angels or emanations and ecstatic experiences of the Most High God are better than Christ. In verse 19 he uses the word *pleroma,* or *fullness* when speaking of Christ as the only true God. *Pleroma* was a technical term used by the Gnostics to reference "spiritual levels of being." Paul is saying that Christ exceeds any level man can invent. In vs. 26, he mentions mystery (*mustering*) to tell of the true mystery that is revealed in Christ—not the mystery of secret knowledge referenced by the Gnostics.

Paul takes another shot at the Gnostics in Colossians 2:3 when he talks about how all the treasures of knowledge (*gnoseos*—a derivative of the word *gnosis* where we get the title Gnostic) are hidden (*apokruphoi*) in Christ. And in a final fatal blow in his all-out attack against the abuses of the Gnostic system, Paul warns the Colossians not to give into their heresy and false teaching in 2:8:

> See to it that no one takes you captive through philosophy and empty deceit, according to human tradition, according to the elemental spirits of the universe *[ta stoicheia tou kosmou]*, and not according to Christ. (NRSV)

The word Paul uses for "elemental spirits" of the world in 2:8 is a similar word to the one Paul uses elsewhere to talk about the "elemental basic teachings" of Christ. Here Paul is saying that the world operates by certain rules, and the kingdom of God operates by a whole different set of rules. Rather than saying we should avoid the world, Paul is saying don't become like them but influence them. He articulates that Jesus' way of life eclipses, overtakes, redeems, and restores the brokenness of the world because it is superior.

He encourages the Colossians to know that Christ is the "fullness of God and that he fills all things," and rather than hating the world and loving only things that we think are spiritual, we need to see that all things are spiritual. Everything in all of creation can be used for good to glorify God. On the opposite end of things, any good thing can be twisted into a god (an item to be worshipped instead of God). We need to learn how to blend two spheres.

30 / THE PSYCHOLOGY (PERSONAL PAIN & MOTIVE)

The problem of the Gnostics continues today. To avoid verbally bashing any one religious system or any particular Christian misuse in specific, let's talk about the sin and psychology of **false teaching** in general. I feel this will help us to better understand how we are all prone to be truth-seeking donkeys chasing after the wrong carrots.

In my work around the world, in now over seventeen countries, and almost the entirety of the United States, I've come to one conclusion concerning my own faith: **I can very easily get sucked into false teaching**. This is true of me, it's true of you, and it's true of everyone that's ever lived, or will ever live. We are humans, we are flesh, and our natural bent apart from Christ is to walk into deception without questions. It's humility to admit our vulnerability. Admitting that we are weak will help us call into question our own beliefs, and I believe it will fill us with an even greater desire to search God's Word. It will drive us to find Bible-believing churches that preach God's Word with the purpose of helping everyone learn its true meaning; rather than simply encouraging people to take and use the Bible however one might wish.

There were many cults, sects, and abusers of truth around in the days of Jesus. Jesus entered our world as flesh and as truth to fully address what's at the heart of all **religious** or **cultic** ways of thinking. In Jesus' day, there were a variety of different religious groups. Listed below are some of the most predominant sects operating in Jesus' region. Together, in essence, they sum up the various directions we all can head in if we believe false teachings:

- **Adding and Restricting:** Pharisees (Tend toward Judgement | Jms. 4:11-12)
- **Reinforcing & Rebellion:** Zealots (Tend toward Rebellion | Psa. 37:30-31)
- **Eliminating & Rejecting:** Essenes (Tend toward Hating the World | Jhn. 17:15)
- **Embracing & Receiving:** Sadducees (Tend toward False Teaching—2 Tim. 4:1-5)
- **Educating & Reading:** Scribes (Tend toward Puffy Pride—1 Cor. 8:1)

First, we like to add things to faith that end up restricting our freedom and the freedoms of others. Pharisees are amazing at this task. They make rules on top of rules. They had taken the written law of God and combined it with their own oral law. They made it impossible for anyone to get into any form of afterlife. They were Grade-A religious. James 4:11-12 explains to us the logical conclusion of someone who lays up rules upon rules:

> Do not speak evil against one another, brothers. The one who speaks against a brother or judges his brother, speaks evil against the law and judges the law. But if you judge the law, you are not a doer of the law but a judge. There is only one lawgiver and judge, he who is able to save and to destroy. But who are you to judge your neighbor?

What James is getting at here is simple. If we add rules of our own to God's law, or we take away from it, we choose ourselves to be the Judge. We prize our sense of justice over God's. When this happens everyone comes under our watching eye. They will either fit into our system or be tossed out; but as James implies, when we set up rules for ourselves, we're the first one to break them. Our rule-setting keeps us from doing the one thing Jesus asked us to do—to love our neighbor, not judge our neighbor.

Adding anything to the simplicity of Jesus will result in Crazy. Jesus + Nothing is the only way that leads to truth.

All religious systems that are false will try to add something to Jesus and his grace in saving us. You can fill in the blank below with what you, your church, your school, or your version of religion might tend to add to Jesus:

$$\text{Jesus} + \text{Nothing} = \text{Truth}$$
$$\text{Jesus} + \underline{\hspace{2cm}} = \text{Crazy}$$

Like the Zealots, we can tend to love developing systems that reinforce our rebellion. The Zealots were the protestors. They were an underground resistance movement. The extremist fighters. They regarded political freedom as a religious imperative. They set up camps, rallies, and anything akin to our modern websites that protest this and that and the other, and they did it under the righteous cry of "No King but God." They rebelled in the name of god, and made god out to be an endorser of their sin and rebellion.

Any system that encourages us to rebel or live in sinfully harmful ways toward others is driven by false teaching.

Like the Essenes, we can tend to separate ourselves by eliminating or rejecting things. The Essenes were a separatist group. Like the Monastics, the Desert Fathers, or various versions of those who are Monks, these Essenes withdrew from the world not for a time, but as the norm. They lived communally. They lived under their own rules. Their flavor of belief resulted in saying things like "the local church isn't holy enough." They worshipped strictly three times a day. They were religiously dutiful. They took ritual baths, bruised their body with deep fasting, and oppressed their people in staunch conservatism.

> *Any system that retreats indefinitely, or encourages us to call one space "sacred" and one space "secular," or embraces the idea that light cannot bring hope to the deepest darkness, is leaning toward false teaching.*

Like the Sadducees, we can tend to embrace and receive things even when they're bad for us. Many will label the Sadducees as "Sad-U-See." Sorry. Bad joke! They were overly conservative. Overly aristocratic. Overly wealthy. Sadducees narrowly received and embraced what they felt was right. They were conservative because they were close minded. They were also very liberal because they were closed-minded. They only let in what they deemed good for them and in doing so, they became bad.

2 Timothy 4:1-5 paints this picture well for us. Timothy writes:

> I charge you in the presence of God and of Christ Jesus, who is to judge the living and the dead, and by his appearing and his kingdom: preach the word; be ready in season and out of season; reprove, rebuke, and exhort, with complete patience and teaching. For the time is coming when people **will not endure**

sound teaching, but having itching ears. **They will accumulate for themselves teachers** to suit their own passions, and will turn away from listening to the truth and wander off into myths. As for you, always be sober-minded, endure suffering, do the work of an evangelist, fulfill your ministry.

Notice the human tendency to embrace, accumulate, or gather to ourselves only people that look like us. We do this when we are unwilling to listen to sound teaching. God claims, and the Bible claims, that truth can only be found in the God-man of Jesus as described in the pages of Scripture. To believe anything else is false teaching.

Any system that says it is seeking truth and yet isolates into communities of people that only "look like them," are showing they've embraced lies.

Lastly, we all can be like Scribes. We are always educating, always reading, and yet never understanding (2 Tim. 3:7). When we learn something, we all tend toward puffy pride. Love on the other end builds people up (1 Cor. 8:1). Puffy pride thinks we've learned the way. Our way is best. Our theology is right. No one disagrees. We hold our position until we meet the thousands that don't see the world the way we do, and we realize how little we actually know.

The Scribes were a little like this. They were copiers and interpreters of the Torah before the exile in 586 BCE. They were the theologians. For them, obedience to the written code wins salvation. The trouble is all the people who were the most learned in Jesus day completely missed that he was coming as a suffering Messiah.

Take Peter, for example. When Jesus asks Peter, "Who do you say I am?" and Peter responds "You're the Christ," we say,

"Okay, he got it, right?" In part, maybe. Jesus does affirm Peter's response in saying, "You can't realize something like that unless the Holy Spirit told you." However, in the very next set of verses, Jesus launches into talking about his own coming death and resurrection, and Peter says, "Absolutely not, you ain't gonna suffer and die," and Jesus says "Get behind me Satan."

Did you catch that? All the learning Peter had had up until that point—all his education at the hand of the Jews—led to a Satanic view of Christ. Many thought Jesus would rule politically. President. Czar. Control. They thought he was going to make them right-hand men. Princes. Sheriffs. Enforcers.

Even after Jesus' death and resurrection they still missed it, and in Luke 24:27 it says that Jesus sat down with them and, "beginning with Moses and all the Prophets, he explained to them what was said in all the Scriptures **concerning himself**." People were always learning and NEVER understanding. Many had the whole Torah memorized, and yet they missed Jesus. Jesus had to take them back through the whole Scripture and reteach them what everything actually meant. Adam, Abraham, Joseph, Moses, Jonah, etc., Jesus took them through story by story and unveiled for them how every story was about himself. Jesus. God. He is love.

Jesus is not puffy pride or just knowledge. Building people up in love and building people up in God is altogether different than just learning something.

> *Any system that makes themselves, anything, or anyone, other than Jesus, central to the goal of education, growth, or especially to understanding the Scriptures, is leaning toward false teaching.*

31 / COMMUNITY PAIN & MOTIVE

The psychology of sin is always looking for a way through and a way out via any other means than Christ. Bottom line. People hate grace. We hate receiving anything we deem charity. We hate receiving something we didn't earn. It makes us feel small. It makes us feel insulted. It makes us feel helpless. We have too much pride. How dare someone think we can't do life on our own? How dare someone say that we're weak? How dare someone judge me and think I need their help?

The real point I'm trying to make in this chapter has really nothing to do with Asher or Gnosticism at all. The psychology of sin forms a community around one thing and one thing only. **Idols.**

Our hearts are constantly spitting out idols. Everything we make begins to make us. Every idol not only comes with its own set of rules, likeness, and flavor, but it presents its own vision of "the good life." It makes a promise. Its slogan makes a sales pitch. If we feel we need what the ad offers, we buy. If we don't feel we need it, we keep walking.

Yet ads don't offend us, but grace does. Ads are constantly saying, "Your life will be better if only you had this." Ads are the best at describing our neediness. They imply that we can't live without their product. Ads present masquerading grace. They are sizing us up, telling us we're smaller than we need to be, and they are promising to make us **bigger**.

Isn't that what any false teaching does? **Makes us bigger**. Asher's school put him one step above. He looked down on the second tier Christians who weren't praying and singing enough. Shekinah's superpowers shrouded her in mystery. They made her the center of attention. They pulled everyone's attention away from God and onto her. When push came to shove, if you were to sit down with Shekinah, you'd see through all the smoke and mirrors. She was just an insecure kid trying to be **bigger**.

Idols make much of us. God makes much of his own glory. God always points back to his story, his actions, and his nature. We point back to ours. The truth is that our endless selfishness isn't helpful. When people start to depend on us we leave them dissatisfied and broken. We let people down. That's our business. That's not God's business. When people turn to God he meets every need perfectly. He's the satisfier of our souls. For him to demand that we praise him, trust him, delight in him, and exalt him over any other idol we might dare to make, is actually the most selfless request he could utter.

Nevertheless, if personalities continue to exalt themselves in ways similar to the Pharisees, the Sadducees, the Zealots, the Essenes, and the Scribes, one of the following types of community will develop:

A мов. When a mob forms they do so out of a demand for something. They do not demand that God be made much of, but they gather more people together to make themselves look **bigger**. "Make much of me," they say. "Do it our way, or else," they'll shout. They will get loud. They will not listen. And why should they, "they are right." Contrast this with the way of Jesus. He was so gentle among us that a bruised reed he did not break and a candle he did not put out.

A POLITICAL PLATFORM. Politics provide a nice place for people to push their views and be liked for it. Whether your platform is liberal or conservative, it doesn't matter. Whether you say you love God or you hate him, doesn't matter. Not anymore anyway. Not in politics. True politics, in how the term is defined today, has nothing to do with God, or so that's what some would have us believe. It has everything to do with man. It's all about how to make man more comfortable, how to preserve more of man's resources, how to enlarge man's army and borders, etc. You get the gist. Political platforms serve only to promote the agendas that man deems "the good life." It makes man **bigger**. Contrast the political mindset with the manner of Jesus. Consider him eating with sinners. Contrast the controlling government aims of today with the governance of heaven and the Kingdom of God. God rules in the human heart. Contrast the big-wigs and their force with the manner of our leader Christ. He considered himself nothing, taking up the very nature of a slave all so he could give us what we need most. He didn't do it to make much of man. He did it in order to restore our ability to feast on the perfections of God.

A SPIRITIST. A Shaman. A Psychic. A Self-Help. Oprah. Dr. Phil. If false teaching is at the center, a personality will become **bigger.** Teachings will get weirder. Out will spring a mob and a political platform. Masses will grow in an effort to bring the truth of "one,"—the minority, to the majority. One might say, isn't Jesus the same? Wasn't he just another prophet, a showman, a Dr. Phil?

The difference? No one has ever claimed to originate from

before time. No one has died, visited the afterlife, resurrected themselves, and proven that they are who they said they were and come back to tell the tale.

Heck, fun fact for those who doubt the difference found in Jesus. Take for example the most unbelievable manner in which our Bible—the life and words of Jesus—were preserved in their original form. One of the ways we know without a doubt that we have the exact words and claims of Jesus in complete accuracy and that he did, in fact, rise again, is via the writings of Atheists. In addition to the over 500 witnesses that saw Jesus after his death, and even those who witnessed his ascension, the atheists and naysayers in that time were so adamant to disprove Jesus' claims along with all eyewitness accounts that they wrote prolifically. We can actually assemble a complete Bible from the writings of atheistic writers trying to disprove what Christ actually did. Unfortunately for the atheists trying to disprove Christ's words and deeds, they actually ended up giving us one of the most reliable records of all that is historical and true.

Thank you atheists for preserving the Christian faith.

The truthful facts of Jesus and the Bible are better than what a guru might offer. Any shaman can only make promises about what's next. Any psychic can't go there themselves and come back with proof. Jesus makes **bigger** claims than anyone that ever lived and yet backs them up in **bigger** ways than anyone ever could. He's the most trustworthy being that's ever lived. He's the most factual. He's the truest and tested hypothesis. We have to call into question and deal with his claims before ruling him out.

THE SYNCRETISTS. These are everywhere. I struggle with being one. We bring our background, culture, preference, biases, and more to the Scriptures, and we approach the Bible like we eat a pizza. We take off what we don't like. We eat what we fancy. This is the community that forms around false teaching. It's a community of nit-picky pizza eaters. It's just a matter of time before pizza-pickers start picking at each other.

At the heart of the syncretist is a desire to be different. To stick out. To be **bigger**. Ironically, in their search to stand out, a syncretist becomes like everyone else. They sync. Pretty soon they fall in amongst everyone else who wants to stick out. Everyone's trying to make a unique statement and so no one does.

Jesus, on the other hand, came into the world and yet is not of the world. He tried quite desperately not to stick out. He intentionally chose the lowliest places and yet has now become the biggest name of all (Phil. 2).

LASTLY, **are the classists.** I've learned, from many years of living in the South and cultures where there is or has been racial tensions, that the greatest issue facing us is classicism, not racism. I have heard well-educated blacks—**bigger**—being called whiggers by uneducated blacks. I've heard upper-class whites called snobs, while lower-class whites are called trash. What the educational classist system of the world has done is created division. It's created planes of existence. Classes. High and Low. It creates bigotry. Different vocations are more valuable and esteemed than others, and celebrities are given credence to rail against injustices they never really experience in their life of privilege. Even celebrities screaming sounds like ignorance to most that are actually poor and oppressed.

In the world today, one's value and relative existence are measured by **information**. Knowledge. If it gets to you, you're empowered and valuable, if it doesn't you're not. It creates planes of being. It's Gnostic, really. On the other hand, once again consider the discipleship model of Jesus. It's altogether different. The last are first. A disciple (a learner) is called a follower not a leader. Christ is the only leader in all of history that says his message is for **all people.** Jesus leveled the playing field for men and women, Jew and Greek, slave and free, sinner and saint. Jesus offered grace to all who would believe.

What the above titles all teach us is that any communal mentality built up and operating around idols will result in the same tragedy. They attempt to make created things **bigger** than the Creator.

The gospel is the remedy. More specifically, the gospel of the kingdom is the remedy. The Kingdom of God operates in complete reverse to that of the world:

In man's kingdom first is best.
In God's kingdom, last are first.

In man's kingdom, the world serves you.
In God's kingdom, you serve the world.

In man's kingdom, resources are dwindling and limited.
In God's kingdom, resources are limitless and always growing.

In man's kingdom, there's death.
In God's kingdom, death ceases.

In man's kingdom, there's suffering, sin, evil, and pain.
In God's kingdom, there's Shalom—peace.

In man's kingdom, people use each other.
In God's kingdom, people build each other up.

In man's kingdom, everything is exclusive and bound by rules.
In God's kingdom, everything is inclusive under God's rule.

In man's kingdom, revenge is justice.
In God's kingdom, forgiveness is justice.

In man's kingdom, the rich are those that take as much as they can.
In God's kingdom, the rich are those that give as much as they can.

On and on the list goes. It becomes quickly apparent whether we're building around the kingdom of man or the kingdom of God. To apply kingdom-grace to a situation that has fallen into false teaching we must only ask ourselves one question; "**Are we making much of man or making much of God?**" We start with what is worshipped as supreme. Everything is answered most deeply by asking the worship question first. Every issue is a worship issue. Centering around the one question of worship can expose false belief, structures, systems, methods, and countless other things that have gone wrong.

When we find ways we have gone astray because of idolatry, we can introduce the reversal of the kingdom into the structures, systems, people, and situations, etc., afforded to us for their own healing and restoration. We can do so simply by introducing the **reversal** of kingdom norms into the chaos of the way the world does things. We can take the high roller and make him/her tend the garden. We can take the pastor who thinks he is bigger than everyone, and watch how he responds when he's made to clean the toilets. Take the teenager who lives a life of privilege and have them work in the slums of Calcutta with no resources. Take the large and in charge self-proclaimed super prophet and make them a student of someone who knows more than they do. Take the spiritist, miracle-seeking Christian and teach them the miracle of service to the fatherless, the oppressed, the orphan, and the widow. Take the musician on stage—strip away their gear—and ask them to go make instruments out of the trash heaps with the extraordinary trash-dump-musicians in Brazil. Assure any fame-monger that they will not be famous for their work.

Ask the taker to give. Take those seeking revenge on their attacker and lead them to forgive. Take the porn addict and help him rescue a little girl from sex trafficking. Ask the liar to tell the truth. Take the cheater back to his wife. Take the one who collapsed in moral failure and put them in a group filled with love and mercy.

All of these redemptive remedies make a person feel **small**. But in God's kingdom, each scenario brings restoration. We are put in our proper place when we feel small before a big God. God's kingdom is all about **reversal.** Making much of God —**bigger**—is the best medicine.

33 / QUESTIONS FOR DISCUSSION

First, contemplate these questions individually and answer in the space provided, and then join together collectively as a group. Here are some Scriptures that can help guide your discussion:

Verses to Consider: *Jms. 2:1-13; Col. 2.*

1. Can you see areas in your own life where you've become an elitist? In other words, where in your life can you see you've subtly created rules, norms, or expectations for people to follow that are not biblical?

2. Can you see how many of those in churches today have bought into the Gnostic way of spirituality?

3. Jesus + Anything = Crazy. What are things you tend to add to

the simplicity of the gospel that can give you a feeling of being a "better-than" Christian?

4. Consider the Zealots, Essenes, Pharisees, Sadducees, and Scribes as mentioned in this chapter. Discuss as a group how you see the propensity of each of these approaches to emerge in yourself and in our culture today.

5. Do you tend toward the mob, the political, the spiritist, the syncretist, or the classist? What motivations do you think drive each one?

6. In what areas do you falsely feel the need to make yourself look *bigger*? What insecurities drive your struggle?

7. In what ways can our families and churches put in place value systems and ways of doing things that aim people toward making much of God, not ourselves?

8. What are some issues going on in the Body of Christ right now that are actually contributing to making people *bigger*? How do we begin to rethink these matters and put in place more helpful kingdom-solutions?

PART 6
BELLS & WHISTLES

34 / THE CASE STUDY

> *... a widespread lack of confidence in Christ's sufficiency is threatening the contemporary church. Too many Christians have tacitly acquiesced to the notion that our riches in Christ, including Scripture, prayer, the indwelling Holy Spirit, and all the other spiritual resources we find in Christ simply are not adequate to meet people's real needs. Entire churches are committed to programs built on the presupposition that the apostles' teaching, fellowship, the breaking of bread, and prayer (Acts 2:42) aren't a full enough agenda for the church as it prepares to enter the ... twenty-first century.*[1]

Bells and Whistles. The latest gear. Sound systems. Lights. Fog. Three-D. The works. Never tell Pastor Quinn that he's not relevant. One can never say that Pastor Q ain't creative.

Pastor Q is just a man's man. By that, I don't mean he is just a meathead. He fits into all of humanity. At least this is the attempt he makes. He's relevant. He's got tattoos, he's ripped and buff, he sports a tiny Apollo trickle of hair under his lip, and his shaved his head makes him even slicker.

Pastor Q talks in slang. He wears jeans, t-shirts, and flip flops in the pulpit. He preaches from an iPad. He stands on a stage furnished with in-ear technology and all the finest gadgets. He lights up his message with gimmicks, props, jokes, vibrant music, quirky skits, and YouTube videos. And this is just when he's at the church.

When he's out and about in the town, you'll never find him without a cigarette or a beer in his hand. Remember, he's relevant. And don't get me wrong, it's not as if having a good brew is forbidden by Scripture—as many Christians falsely believe—but Pastor Q is different. His conversation is filled up with a discussion about beer. His obsession with it almost makes one wonder, "Is this all he talks about?" It makes the Christian bring to mind the Scripture that says, "Be filled with the spirit, not with drink and wine." Though Pastor Q never gets drunk, it sure seems like the topic of drinking **fills** up more conversations than does his talk of God.

Then there's Rustic Creek Church. If one thinks Pastor Q is relevant, RCC is known for being more than relevant. Every Halloween they give out more candy, more video games, more carnival rides, and more experiences than anyone in town. Their kid's ministry is hopping. They dirt bike. Motor-cross. Race cars. Fish. Mountain bike. Rock Climb. You name it. They do it.

The only thing not relevant about RCC is Earl. Earl is Pastor Q's Dad. He's ol'-fashioned. To Pastor Q, Earl is out of touch. Trouble is, Earl is on staff as one of the co-pastors of RCC. Pastor Q and Earl are constantly in disagreement, and yet no one can ever tell. Pastor Q and Earl speak to each other cordially in all matters and yet underneath their pleasantry is a sea of waves and storms. Earl zips his lips as Pastor Q runs over him. Pastor Q rolls his eyes behind closed doors at everything his dad says because let's face it, Earl is not relevant.

Earl is old. He's simple. He believes the church meets in

homes, and that the kingdom often shows up powerfully in just sitting next to the dying and cancer-ridden down in the local hospital. Earl's heart is as big as the hills and as deep as the mountain lakes. He's a counselor. He's a people person. You'll never see him on stage, and there's not a person in town who has not shared a meal with him. He's not relevant, and yet he's loving. Everyone knows Earl whereas no one knows the real Pastor Q.

For Pastor Q, ministry tends to rely on all things **seen.** For Pastor Earl, well, let's just say there's hardly a moment that he's not working behind the scenes doing the **unseen**.

---

[1] MacArthur, J. Jr. *Our Sufficiency in Christ* (Wheaton, IL: Word Publishing, 1998), 19.

THE STORY

The king of Aram is a violent man. He's a raiding man. He's a spoiled man.

What does God do to spoiled men?

Let's find out …

Each time the Syrians try to defeat Israel, their plans are foiled by God through Elisha (2 Kgs. 6:11). The text in 2 Kings tells us that the king of Aram becomes so paranoid and infuriated that he accuses his soldiers of being traitors and silent servants to the king of Israel. In response, one of the officers simply replies, "None of us are on the side of Israel … but Elisha, the prophet who is in Israel, tells the king of Israel the very words you speak in your bedroom" (vs. 12).

One can only picture the king of Aram falling back aghast. White as a sheet. Lifeless. Angry. Betrayed. Hostile. How dare this Elisha play him the fool with some magic trick?

In shy confidence and insecurity, the king tries to preserve his image of strength. He swears, "Where is this so-called 'servant of god,' who can see into my bedroom?" In making an inference, one may assume what might be swirling around inside the king's head: *"This God sees me in my chambers? What else does Elisha know? What about that secret I have ..."*

Regardless of any uncertainty still remaining in the king, the men leave to find Elisha in the city of Dothan, while the king stays back to chew on his fear and intimidation. The men streak across the countryside with chariots, horses, and strong forces. They surround the city by night. Close to dawn, one of the servants to Elisha breaks into his chambers; "An army. Oh no, my lord! What shall we do?"

Elisha responds, "Don't be afraid ... those who are with us are more than those who are with them."

What does Elisha mean by his statement "We are more than those?" Is Dothan a military base? Is the city strong enough? The servant pauses to wonder, "Who is he talking about ... what armies ... me? You?"

But Elisha does not reveal in words that to which he references in his hidden trust. Elisha fails to make known any attack plan. Elisha refuses to simply pull out some new methodology that can make things all better. Elisha knows that moving around frantically only proves insufficient; as useless as the fear that the servants currently are feeling. Elisha knows that most new methods are motivated by fear—**in what is seen**—rather than by faith—**what is unseen**. Elisha knows the human tendency all too well: the tendency to grasp for **the bigger and the better** in moments of perceived weakness, instead of trust that **more is already there.**

Elisha responds. He **prays**:

"O Lord, please open his eyes that he may see." So the Lord opened the eyes of the young man, and he saw, and behold, the mountain was full of horses and chariots of fire all around Elisha. And when the Syrians came down against him, Elisha prayed to the Lord and said, "Please strike this people with blindness."

Elisha is a man with eyes of faith, not sight. Elisha is a man of old, not new gadgets. Elisha cries out. Elisha perceives. Elisha intuits a battle that rages far beyond the reach of human technologies like swords, spears, shields, and chariots. In response to Elijah's faith, the servant is allowed to see what many of us will never see, *the host of angels at the ready.*

The armies of heaven stand by to fight a war that is never Elisha's to fight. Frankly, kings of Aram are not new. There have been thousands of men like him before, and there will be thousands still. The battle-hungry King of Aram is nothing but another king hoping to wage war against the kingdom of God and his people.

Hezekiah later faces the same thing against the Assyrian armies, and Elisha conveys the same truth to him as he does here to the servant against the Syrians; "Be strong and courageous, do not fear or be dismayed because of the king of Assyria, nor because of all the multitude which is with him; for the one with us is greater than the one with him. With him is **only** an arm of flesh, but with us is the Lord our God to help us and to fight our battles" (2 Chr. 32:7-8). Elisha perceives that there is an arm of flesh and an arm of faith that comes in any battle. The arm that is **made** in flesh may certainly benefit from the arms made in **faith**, but flesh certainly does nothing useful on its own.

36 / THE PSYCHOLOGY (PERSONAL PAIN & MOTIVE)

The fear that motivated the sightless servant in the story of Elisha motivates many of the Pastor Q's in our day. Let me very quickly clarify what I do not mean by this statement. What I'm not attempting to do is condemn. I'm not attempting to launch into a long conservative, anti-tech rant about how we should not use all the tools afforded to us in order to be effective for God's kingdom in this world. One of the businesses I own is a tech and innovation company, so I would be condemning myself. Whether our creative innovations are shields, swords, bows, arrows, and chariots, or whether they happen to be lights, projectors, curriculum, legal documents, research, paint brushes, bald heads, or tattoos, I say we use all things redemptively to see people meet God.

However, I also think we need to use caution and great wisdom. Wisdom is the first thing to go out the door when following the "cult of cool." C. S. Lewis commented on the newness of cool when he said something to this effect, "The end of man is going to be doing all that he imagines." We're created by our Creator and are by nature innovative, and yet if we set out to do all we imagine and dream of, it will assuredly be the end of us. The Tower of Babel is an example of this.

The Tower of Babel was the coolest thing in its day. It was akin to Elon Musk's Tesla in space, a man walking on the moon, satellites, and the Hubble Space Telescope. The Tower of Babel reached the top of the world. And for what purpose? The people dreamed up the tower out of a desire to have the world make much of them. They wanted to have people say "Look at them."

Self-centered fame is at the heart of every human not in submission to Christ. We all can tend to struggle in one of two directions with our prideful god-complex: one direction I call the "Jeff Bezos Syndrome" and the other direction I coin as the "Elon Musk Complex." Jeff Bezos, founder of Amazon is always unclear in what his real purpose behind his company is, but in all his practices we see one thing—lordship. He leans toward the idea of control. Everything ends with him. Elon Musk is quite different. He's the rescuer. He's the Savior. He's the one that's going to bring us off this planet into a better world.

Augustine used to say that every believer bows to Christ two times in their life, one as Savior, and the other as Lord. Our tendency as humans is to try and become either of these ourselves, but Jesus is the Savior and the Lord, and he holds the vision of our rescue and he also holds the universe under his control.

My mention of Amazon and Tesla may seem like a long rant about nothing, but I think it goes a long way into uncovering the psyche of our sin, particularly in the case of Pastor Q and the unseeing servant with Elisha. Our drive to be relevant is admitting that we feel God is not relevant. But the gospel is ALWAYS relevant.

We carry within our grasp the only good news that can transform and bring life into the world in any era or decade. Nevertheless, we begin to think that gadgets, toys, light shows, and big bangs show forth the glory of "god" better than he can himself. The toys all too often quickly eclipse the community. The seen becomes prized and more valuable than the unseen. Practicality replaces mystery. Pragmatics replace story and imagination, and in striving to become more "relevant," we simply become like everyone else. We get sucked up in our quest to exert ourselves as either Savior or Lord.

It happens subtly. It happens when we do everything we imagine and all of a sudden our churches grow beyond complex. Our environments start to undermine the very gospel we preach. We start to become organizations, not organisms. We lose family in the swells of corporate. We are efficient but far less patient. We have goals, mission statements, and big visions, and yet subtly we lose the love within moments.

Pastor Q set out with good intentions, as do we all. He wanted to harness the power of the **made** to tell people about their **Maker.** He wanted the **created** to point to a **Creator.** In defense of the right use of creativity, I say yes, and Amen. However, there comes a point where our **tools** begin making us. I'll explain what I mean by this in deeper fashion in talking about the remedy, and the healing that must take place in all our "relevant" leaders out there, but for now, let's consider what this does to a community.

37 / COMMUNITY PAIN & MOTIVE

If you'll permit me to make examples of people once more, let me poke respectively at the late Steve Jobs and the mass hysteria over phones, computers, and wireless gadgets of all shapes and sizes. The reason I want to take a look at what I call "The Theology of Technology" is not to condemn it. Even as we speak, I am writing on my MacBook Pro, texting with my iPhone, and all are being stored in my iCloud, so it's no secret that I love Apple products—but I want to think theologically for a second. I want to encourage us to be mindful makers, consumers, and users of the tools that are making us. I believe that the iPhone is a very great case example of how a small idea can utterly shape, capitalize on, and even affirm and prey upon all of humanities' deepest weaknesses.

ALL OF LIFE is a doxological response (giving praise and honor to something we prize), and everything to which we put our hands reflects our beliefs. Apple is no different. Whatever we deem to be the most praiseworthy "thing," we will sacrifice for it, we will be shaped by it, formed by it, and we can ultimately end up reflecting on what it has to teach us. The iPhone like any created thing can be good, but its creation is driven by the theological principles and beliefs of the one making it. Apple continues to use language in its invention that I believe causes detrimental shifts in our culture and the way we behave. I think understanding Apple's theology is important.

Apple is shaping culture into their image.

I am particularly susceptible to the shaping power of Apple. I have a problem, and Apple can become my cocaine of choice. I'm addicted to ideas. I love to create fantastical dreams in my head of imaginary visions and future conquests. Why not? It's like a video game! It makes me feel bigger than I am; it "super-heroizes" me into a victor.

Vision and ideas can be helpful because they help us imagine things that are beyond us, but if our hope is anchored solely in these things—these lesser pleasures—it can be the end of us. What if our dream or idea doesn't pan out? In Scripture, we've been promised a hope that is sure and dependable. Hebrews 6:19 says, "We have this as a sure and steadfast anchor of the soul, a hope that enters into the inner place behind the curtain …" This verse promises Christians the ability to apprehend the kingdom of God in the NOW through Jesus who has torn the veil between us and heaven. Though there is more to come when Jesus fully brings us into his prepared place in the NOT YET, we await an ideal, a utopia, and a preferred future that Jesus promises is coming! His promise is not breakable or fleeting, but sure.

Apple inadvertently plays off humanity's need to imagine ideas and to think of things beyond their pay grade. They paint a future that is bright, expanding, and a kingdom for which we hope. I love watching Apple KeyNote talks as the salivating crowd perches on the edge of their seats to await their future, but let's remember that our future is filled with Jesus—a much bigger presence than Apple.

Apple creates a preferred world for most people. Their big push is story and narrative. Their brand capitalizes on the fact that they can connect the world's story cohesively through individuals by harvesting everyone's creativity to be shared in a vast network that can ultimately give human innovation purpose, platform, and community. The idea of story is good, but we must remember who the central character is. In any good story, there exists a main character. If the author fails to establish that character, the story falls flat. This is why the Bible is written in story and narrative. God wanted to tell a story that is full of tension, climax, denouement, turning points, and plot twists. God created us for story, and the plot twists of the Bible reflect our place within the narrative.

In Jesus' time, the religious leaders of the day got the story all wrong as well. So much so, that when Jesus came along the disciples thought that Jesus was going to be a political king and that they were going to be his henchmen. Unfortunately, they had read the story of scripture wrong and thought that it was about them, their superiority, and their perfect observance of the law. I mentioned in an earlier chapter Luke 24:27. After Jesus rises from the dead, we are told that the disciples were still profoundly confused about who Jesus was, what the Old Testament was for, and who they were supposed to be, and it tells us that this is what Jesus did: "And beginning with Moses and all the Prophets, he interpreted to them in all the Scriptures the things concerning himself."

That's right, the story of Scripture was, is, and always will be about Jesus, and without knowing the main character, the whole interpretation of God's work is off balance. How much more so is a world that sees through Apple glasses and believes that our story is the supreme contribution to the universe? It seems that before we create our story we must get to know the main player of whose story we're in better. Jesus gets to decide what is beneficial to his narrative, not us, and certainly not Apple!

Apple technology continues its attempt to define, shape, and craft character and belief. It forms our belief of what a god should be.

Let's ponder the apps for just a moment. If you touch an app, you expect it to move at warp speed, right? If it doesn't connect you to what you want faster, more efficiently, and with greater ease than it did in its previous version, then you, and I for that matter, throw a tantrum. We yell when the internet takes .5 seconds to load, we pay thousands more just to increase our storage drives and memory for faster connection and delivery, and we expect the iPhone, in conjunction with Google search, to connect us to what we need, when we need it—right now!

This shapes our character. Consider the Bible's talk on forbearance, long-suffering, steadfastness, and slowness. One of the fruits of the Spirit is patience, and Apple seems to be convincing us that this is not a virtue, but a vice. Our tools are actually targeting the "fruit of the spirit." They are warring to replace the character of Christ in us with the nature of the world.

Tools have the power to morph how we see God. When we pray, we think he should react on our terms as fast as our app does. When we need direction, we expect him to move heaven and earth and to sovereignly Google all the answers right before our eyes—as if we expect him to literally write his answer across the glassy sky. The theology of all technology is un-shaping Christian character and shaping our view of what god should be like. Theological and scriptural grounding is necessary to be able to use these techie tools to our advantage and not to our detriment.

Let's also consider Apple's view of beauty. If you're around Apple for five minutes, you'll hear a stream of catchphrases, jargon, and pitches that are all outlined by the word "beauty." It's no secret that Steve Jobs had taste, and his stroke of genius is not merely in the invention of the products, but in his ability to make them cool. I will forever affirm Steve Jobs' biblical desire for excellence.

However, Apple has restricted beauty to how something looks and feels, and it has forever made the word "beautiful" into something that is physical and functional. They capitalize on the portrayal by others, like Playboy, sleazy sitcoms, and others, who depict men and women only as important if they are physically beautiful.

What about Jesus' affirmation of the culturally pitiful display of the women anointing him with oil, as he says in Matthew 26:10, "She has done a beautiful thing to me"? What about Jesus' condemnation of the Pharisees who were "like whitewashed tombs, which outwardly appear beautiful, but within are full of dead people's bones and all uncleanness"? What about Peter's insistence that true beauty was not in outward adornment, but in inward quietness and class? I'm not saying that Apple does not make good products, but can they hijack a term like beauty and redefine it in a way that God would not?

The Apple watch plays off the misuse of the term beauty, and its catchphrase is "Beauty at a glance." It wants to create a personalized world for those with even less time. But what's the difference between a glance and a gaze? In Psalm 24:7, David longs to do nothing else but gaze upon the beauty of the Lord. In a glance, one can only grab what one wants, but in a gaze, one contemplates the beauty, the perfection, and the extravagance of another.

With the rise of the Apple Watch, Apple is redefining personalized and making "personal" what we get from an object rather than the beauty of the object itself. This is theologically cancerous! True beauty and creation is no longer that which is contemplated and gazed upon in appreciation, delight, and with the sole desire of enjoying the object of our affections—which produces love—but beauty and love are now cast as mere things that can be obtained in our timeframe, on our clock (literally), and as quickly as we say. Our need-it-my-way mentality is perfect for a friends-with-benefits culture, wouldn't you say?

We assume now that to know someone should be as personalized, quick, and nifty as the watch itself. It affects how we love others. More appropriately worded, it influences how we neglect to love others. Facebook has already turned friendship into a number, Twitter has already turned poetry into a hashtag, and Tinder has turned sex into a toy … Is Apple now turning knowing someone into jewelry? Are "persons" now only for display, like a man carrying a hot blonde as a trophy to affirm his masculinity and fame? We must think long and hard about the words we are using to describe things. Apple is creating good things, using good language, and attaching them to each other in all the wrong ways. I shudder at the day when "to know someone" is actually to depersonalize them.

APPLE HAS FORMED A COMMUNITY. They have reinterpreted words, changed meanings, and have given the world a brand new way to relate to each other. Did you catch that? **Brand new.** Their new ideas have literally turned heads. People no longer look at each other, they bow their heads before their almighty Phone. And in a world that claims to be **the most social** and global culture to have ever existed in the world's history, we are **living alone together** because of the tools we've made.

Instead of throwing stones at one another and their creations, let's bring this back on ourselves as we push toward a gospel remedy. Let's expose how the church has subtly started to lose ground in culture-shaping and have actually lost ourselves to some degree in the cult of the brand new. To do this, let me briefly back track to the beginning of the church. To the beginning of time, actually. Let's talk briefly about what's now become "ole hat," too simple, not relevant, and too out of touch. Let's talk about the simplicity of God's technology. The simplicity that our complex innovations often threaten to draw us away from the most. The meal.

FIRST OF ALL, isn't it interesting that the whole storyline of Scripture is built around meals? God uses meals as a paradigm for how we're to think about his kingdom advancement and embrace, but also as a symbol of blessing and cursing. Consider this small list of just a few of the turning points in Scripture where blessing or cursing coincides with and takes place around a meal:

- God's blessing began in the garden with a meal (Gen. 1:29).
- God gave Adam and Eve a choice to eat of blessing or curse, symbolized in the Tree of Life and Tree of Knowledge of Good and Evil.
- The curse, fall of mankind, and Satan's temptation happened over a meal (Gen. 2:16-17).
- The first family struggle, over a food offering, resulted in murder. Cain and Abel (Gen. 4).
- In the Flood, God preserved animals and food for Noah's family as blessing and destroyed everyone else as a sign of curse (Gen. 7:1-3).
- The first burnt offering and declaration of clean and unclean food (Gen. 9:3-4).
- The beginning fulfillment of the promise made to Abraham is made over a meal (Gen. 18:2).
- Jacob deceives Esau over food (Gen. 25).
- Joseph's rise to power is during a famine, and Joseph's wise reign leads to provision for all (Gen. 37-52).
- God's work in freeing his people from the Egyptians is remembered in the Passover meal (Exo. 12).
- God provides manna for his people in wandering (Numbers).
- Ruth, through whose lineage would come King David, was provided for, betrothed, and kept alive by Boaz through gleanings of wheat (Ruth).
- Daniel refused to eat from Nebuchadnezzar's table and asked to continue in his freedom to eat as God had instructed (Dan. 1:8).
- God's sovereign rule and the deliverance of the entire Jewish nation in the Book of Esther comes over a meal (Purim—Esther).

- Jesus enters his ministry and is tempted with food (Luk. 4).
- Jesus' ministry is spent attending Jewish Feasts (Jhn. 2) and feeding people (Mrk. 6:30-44).
- When "all authority in heaven and earth is given to Jesus," in his last moments before the cross, he chose to hold the Last Supper (Luk. 22:7-23).
- The church begins, forms, and grows over meals (Acts 2:42).
- Meals are used to symbolize fake religion or true freedom (Col. 2:20-23).
- Weak and Strong faith is contrasted through the metaphor of eating (Rom. 14).
- Heaven on Earth (The Final kingdom) is portrayed as Table Fellowship, around a Tree of Life, at the Wedding Supper of the Lamb (Rev. 19:6-9).

Every time God initiates something in the timeline of history, it is done in and around a meal. Meals are the foundation to Jesus's ministry, the life of the local church, and should be the paradigm of simplicity that we need to recapture today. Let's consider Jesus as a foremost example.

Theologians have noted in Luke's Gospel, that there is not a moment where Jesus is not going to, at a, or coming from a meal. The sinners who knew Jesus met him as a "friend of sinners" at meals, and Jesus' enemies were always at odds over the fact that he kept eating with sinners. The famous historian and doctor, Luke, kept alive the rhythm of meals and their symbol as a blessing or curse. Jesus used meals as a visual display to demonstrate his desire to invite all men, women, and children to his table. If a person accepted or declined his invitation to eat, their answer symbolized a desire to either come inside Christ's kingdom or to remain on the outside.

The Early Church continued the tradition of eating. In fact, in the first three centuries, largely up until the time that Constantine politicalized Christianity as the state religion, the whole of the Christian worship service (the gathering) was referred to as "the Lord's Supper." It wasn't a wafer and a sip from a plastic throw-away cup that was in Paul's mind in 1 Corinthians 10:17-34 when he speaks of the Supper. The context of Paul's argument in 1 Corinthians clearly regards the church service as being a full meal that was substantial enough to satisfy hunger. It was clearly a meal in which everyone had a part, and it was a meal weighty enough in length of time, to where the rich and poor were allowed enough leeway to develop considerable relational issues.

Not only were meals crucial for forming a community but they actually were a "video image" of the kingdom of God. Let me explain. There's a theological term for how early people believed God to interact with each other in a similar manner as the Trinity. Later in history, a theological term emerged to describe the view … *perichoresis*. It implies that our God is in a circle and dancing. The imagery of God's face-to-face dance originates from John 1, where he says, "in the beginning was the Word (Jesus), and the Word was **with** God, and the Word was God." This word "with" explains how God faces himself. Our God is in a circle. They are staring at each other in joyful love. A dance.

The early Christians met this way in the early days. They gathered in circles. In fact, most of the paintings we have that depict early church life show circles of people, meeting in homes, sitting around meals. And yet, after Constantine, we can visibly see a change in church architecture over the next 2,000 years. Building started getting longer. Rectangular. Leaders started getting further away from congregations. Stages started developing. Leaders began looking down on congregations not across and at them. Pews were fashioned to face the front, not each other. We now relate to screens, not faces. Modern technological jargon calls it FACETIME.

Why is noting the change so important?

Foremost, our environments now undermine our message. The cult-of-cool and all that is new has mesmerized us so avidly that we've walked headlong into methods that actually pull us away from our roots. We preach from hard pulpits, raised stages, cold street corners, and the like, and we talk using **family words**. We talk about the household and Bride of God. We call Jesus our husband and brother, God our Father, and the Holy Spirit our helper and one called alongside (the image of a mother). We speak words that do not match our environments. We stand on stages and say "it's not about the stage." We call Pastors "Senior" and yet say it's not about the man. We call the guitar-playing tenor the "Worship Leader" and say that "worship is not all about music." What is shown and what is spoken sit in contradiction. The church really is simply struggling with improper use of the game **show and tell**.

Meanwhile, the simplicity of the home and the Lord's Supper is really ludicrous to most; yet the home, meal, and the marriage is the only environment that actually matches the message of the gospel in the fullest sense. The message of the gospel is not just spoken in words but is seen in the worlds that we create for people to live in. Through our very new and innovative ideas, we've actually created for ourselves most of our current problems.

Along similar lines, this is why I find it fascinating that God did not start the creation in the context of a 501(c3) non-profit, a building, a cabinet, a district, a board, or an institution of any kind. God saw fit to share his love with the world and to multiply his image on earth within the context of a garden, through the relationship of a man and a woman in a marriage, and in a family. In Genesis 1:29 God inaugurates his mission on earth with a meal.

God's wise method for making himself known on the earth with something as simple as soil, meals, and a family is brilliant. Why?

The first reason is that God is timeless (outside of and unbound by limits) and can see the beginning of time as well as the ending. It would seem logical that God not only saw our "today" while creating the world in Genesis—and in deciding how he would sovereignly layout, orchestrate, and assemble the known creation—but he also saw the church, wars, pestilence, persecution, famine, power struggles, and all the other countless evils that were going to spring upon the earth as a result of our sickness and sin.

Hypothetically speaking, this must have caused God to ask himself something to this effect: "With all the hostility seeking to stop my plans, promises, purposes, and people on the earth, I must put into place a paradigm for ministry that can survive in any time, in any place, and under any circumstance." In God choosing to advance his image and love on the earth through meals, he shows us his wisdom.

Eating and drinking are timeless methods of showing the Triune nature of our God. They are both necessary to life, and meals are the one thing that brings creation (garden) and family together in a manner that both are included in the gospel message of redemption, and in a way that makes the gospel both visible and invisible. The broken creation is masterfully whipped together into recipes of order that taste of beauty. Redemption! All of humankind dines relationally and in face-to-face unity and service toward one another—a passionate community of togetherness. Redemption! God restores our ability to be "with" one another in the meal. In the time of the iPhone where everyone's neck is crooked downward toward their device, we've lost the art of being with one another.

After reading all this, can we begin to see the truth of C. S.

Lewis' words? Once again his prediction was that our end will come in doing everything we imagine. Much of what we've called innovation over the last two thousand years has actually taken us away from the home, has caused us to lose the simplicity of meals together, and has actually led to mental illness, broken families, anxious and worn out people, activity-exhausted parents, divided up ministries claiming to bring family and generations together, and kids who lack a sense of belonging. A sense of belonging is disappearing from our churches.

In an attempt to prescribe a gospel remedy to the new-fangled bells and whistles that have silenced the church into relation-less consumption, rather than equipped us toward communal production, I'm starting to wonder if all we're doing as the church is doing more to slow us down over and above building us up.

The remedy to our cult-of-the-new is to come back to our consideration of the traditions of old. We need a balance between the invention of today and the traditions of yesterday. Both/And. Though nothing is perfect and everything comes with its complications (if you don't believe me, just read about the mealtimes of the Corinthians), we need to make a decision about what problems are worth dealing with. Largely, the problems that come from meeting in meals, marriages, and homes bring about issues of us **getting too close**. In the models of church work today, many of the problems we deal with every day are addressing how **we've grown too far away** from one another.

If given a choice in innovation, I particularly consider it an honor to create backward into simplicity rather than forward into complexity. I for one revel in the joys and problems that result from people **being too close** over and above trying to deal with all the issues of people **being too far away**.

QUESTIONS FOR DISCUSSION

F irst, contemplate these questions individually and answer in the space provided, and then join together collectively as a group. Here are some Scriptures that can help guide your discussion:

Verses to Consider: *Ecc. 1:9-11, 5:1-3, 12:9-14.*

1. What fascinates us about what is *new*? Why are we so captivated with the *seen*, when so much of our life is dependent on the *unseen* (e.g. gravity, air, etc.)?

2. C. S. Lewis states, to put it nicely, "that our imaginations will be the end of us?" What he means is that we often dream up things that aren't particularly helpful, but they may seem cool. How do we engage our imagination unto God's glory and only put into place the ideas that preserve his simplicity?

. . .

3. If you were to envision legions of angels guarding you right now in the ***unseen*** realm, how would that change the way you live practically today?

4. Does question #3 expose any in you where you have grown distrustful of God; having turned toward worldly methods to accomplish your goals?

5. In what ways have you seen the "tools we've made" making you?

6. How can we redeem the tools of our world so that they drive us back to God's models for discipleship (centered around the home, meal, and family)?

7. Today, even our church *environments* undermine our message in many unhelpful ways. How can we begin to provide solutions to this issue and begin to help our environment match our message?

8. God intends that our way of doing things should work *in any time, in any place, and under any circumstance.* Why did God set up paradigms instead of methods to preserve this? How have many of our "new ways of doing things" actually hurt us, not helped us?

PART 7
I'LL BLOW YOUR HOUSE DOWN

THE CASE STUDY

Shrewd. Wise. Thoughtful. Theological. Calculated. Prayerful. These are all words that describe Noah. Noah took the plunge several years ago to move from the conservative culture of a little town in Texas into the mass liberal hysteria of Boston, MA. His little town in Texas is very different from that of Boston. Texas is filled with people who are moral and label it as Christianity. Many struggle with being judgmental and bound by rules and calling it faith. In many cases, this is the sad end to all conservatism. Values get misused in order to build fortresses rather than bridges. They keep people out rather than letting people in. Noah feels trapped in the fortresses. He feels that when those in his community are invited to interact with the sinner, the lost, the destitute, the partier, and the broken son far from home, they simply decline the invitation.

Noah loves all persons because God does. However, Noah's heart is for the Prodigal, not the Pharisee. Even though both are desperate for God, Noah spends all his time in ministry reaching those much like the "older brother" in his little town. He wants to take a deeper dive into a culture that actively walks away from God in tangible, rebellious ways.

Upon arriving into liberal Boston, MA, Pastor Noah dedicates himself to building bridges with people rather than fortresses. Noah puts on the clothes of those in Boston. He sports a button-up untucked shirt with a loose tie and a fedora upon his head. He prefers jeans that look like they've already been worn and muddied, and he laces up the latest Converse low-top shoes just to top off the metro-casual style.

Noah frequents the town pubs in order to meet people. He hangs around the Boston College campus in order to participate in lively and spirited conversations about the nature of God's existence and to learn how people are defining truth these days. Noah discovers what he set out to find. He finds the academic and the life-style prodigals.

Within a short year of his arrival, Redemption City Church is born. About seventy newly saved prodigals gather each and every week right across from the Boston College campus to worship, pray, and hear God's Word together. Pastor Noah is right where he aimed to be; surrounded by newly journeying skeptics of the faith. Noah presses in hard to the people in order to help them learn truth.

But Noah is alone. He feels it. Like Moses in need of Jethro's advice, Noah quickly seeks the Lord for help in the area of discipling the people. Everyone coming is full of questions. Hard questions. Skeptical questions. The kind of questions that require one to soak deep time in study, prayer, and many hours of discussion. Though Noah loves the growth happening, the people bend his ear far too much. His ear begins to break. His back begins to give. He cannot carry the load himself of this deeply, passionate, growing group of young Christians. Noah becomes weak. He's tired. He's increasingly insecure about his ability to handle such a responsibility.

In comes Ben and Keith. They're unassuming but soldiers of truth in civilian clothes. Noah can tell they are seasoned and can handle the Word of God like the sword that it is. They're trained. They were born and raised to be believers. Both carry Ph.D.s in Philosophy and Theology. They're already friends. To Noah, they are heroes.

Like a dried up horse looking for an oasis in the desert, Noah clings to Ben and Keith like a life preserver. Ben and Keith step up to the challenge and begin to serve Noah much like Aaron had Moses; holding up his arms in the battle of discipling those at Redemption City Church.

Mere weeks pass and Ben and Keith become elders along with Noah. Together these three men and their three families shoulder the passionate and growing community of RCC.

As the church nears a hundred people after just under a year of the journey, things start to get a little messy. Ben continues on faithfully, but Keith starts to show signs of veering from the truth. He starts to question the core doctrines of Church practice. Detours are a common mistake amongst philosophers and off he goes. Like all good speculators, Keith begins to dream up new ideas and puts into words thoughts he's entertained for a long time that are straight-up weird.

Whereas Ben lets his theology take the lead and have authority over his philosophy, Keith is vice versa: Keith's philosophy overtakes his theology. If theology is like the lines drawn on a soccer field in order to encourage the free and vibrant interaction of the players, Keith throws out the lines and in turn creates a whole new game. Chaos.

Keith's faith loses all orthodoxy. He becomes increasingly vocal. Loud. Bitter. He is loose with answers and questions and quickly becomes a protestor, not an advocate.

Noah and Ben approach Keith over his actions and apparent rebellion toward truth. Keith only laughs. He tosses his head back in annoyance and continues on in tossing truth out the window. People follow him. The church divides. A mess of brokenness, bitterness, and torn families follow. Redemption City Church and Keith come to an impasse. Keith and all his followers leave.

Redemption City dwindles down to about twenty people, whereas Keith begins Seeker Church just about two blocks away. Almost everyone follows Keith and calls it a "revival" and the "change needed." Seeker Church is a church based around the idea that all supposed truth is to be held in question. Keith prioritizes the ability of the mind to discern its own truth. The Bible is no longer taught. Seeker Church becomes yet another testimony to how one can call something a church while it is nothing but a cult.

Redemption City Church reels in the aftermath of this **wolf in sheep's clothing**. Noah paces his office, the neighborhood, and the stage of the church just trying to figure out what he missed. Noah blames himself for allowing a wolf to come in and feast on the sheep of God. He'd been snowed by Keith's wit, degree, and charm. Underneath Keith bore nothing but fangs scraping after the pigs saying "Come out, come out, or I'll huff, and I'll puff, and I'll blow your house down."

41 / THE STORY

The story of Noah and Keith is nothing new. Wolves have always taken advantage of God's sheep. In the day of Moses and Aaron the people of God experienced this same pull toward false teachers and teachings in the people of Moab, and in and through the words of a false Prophet named Balaam.

The Book of Numbers tells the famous story of Balaam and the talking donkey. Interestingly enough, most of the Book of Numbers is about Israel's journey toward the Promised Land, but in chapters 22-24 the focus shifts and begins to detail what transpires within the other nations as Israel traverses through the land. In Numbers 22:1-19 the camera zooms out and pans left to capture what is going on in another nation—the nation of Moab.

The biblical record introduces four major characters in the story of God's enemies: Balak, the Messengers, Balaam, and the Moabite Princes. In the story, Balak's kingdom reflects the kingdom of evil and its pride that wars against God and his people. We learn that Satan's rule has real kings (like Balak), real false prophets (Balaam), real princes, and real messengers and missionaries. Balak represents an opposing power to the people of

Israel and to God, and as the antagonist character within the story, he is pitted in comparison against the leadership style of Moses. Balak, as the overseer of his people, leads them in a similar fashion to Moses. He is entrusted to protect his people. As Moses seeks his direction from the LORD, Balak seeks out guidance from evil sources. He is an evil king. Though Moses is a very meek and humble leader who leads in righteousness and draws from a holy and powerful source in Yahweh, Balak is a man of pride and wicked intent.

Balak's thinking in regard to himself is filled up with idle notions of his own power and ownership of the land. He falls prey to the belief that everything is his. In Numbers 22:6, his view of himself grows so detached from reality that he claims for himself and his nation the promises that God made to Abraham and Israel. He believes that God is on his side to bless all those he blesses and to curse all those he curses. He acts on false belief and assumption not only in thought but also in action.

Balaam and the party of messengers are not altogether different than Balak. Whereas Balak masquerades as a king, Balaam is a spiritist masquerading as a Prophet. Balak comes to seek Balaam's blessing against the Israelites and Balaam appears only interested in the money he will receive for his services. In fear that the King will discover that Balaam is a shyster and liar, thus withdrawing the handsome payment, Balaam sets up a smoke-and-mirror show. He pretends to speak to the God of the Bible on behalf of Balak.

Surprisingly in the story, we are told that God answers Balaam's rude attempts to parade around in false truths while all dressed up in lies. Though the true God of the universe gives Balaam instructions, the story leads us to this one amazing scene where the real motives of Balaam are revealed. As Balaam travels along to meet Balak, an angel stands in Balaam's way, causing his donkey to veer, stir, get anxious, and try to find a way around. In anger, Balaam strikes the donkey, and the donkey speaks to him saying: "What did I ever do to you?"

The irony of the story is that the only truthful character in the plot is an **ass.** The donkey is the only person, place, or thing that even acknowledges the angel in its way. He's honestly the only thing in the story portrayed as one who "seeks the truth."

All of this is instructive in how evil, false teaching, and false teachers act in Scripture and in history. In their attempts to play everyone else off as the fool, they come out looking like asses. In trying to disprove truth, or in mocking it in some way, they merely dig their own graves. The truth of God ends up humiliating them.

Consider the story of Balak in light of the Book of Revelation. It has always been a common tactic of Satan to try and imitate or counterfeit things in order to make things appear to be as God, or from God. As in the case of the counterfeit "Trinity" created in Numbers in the structure of Balak (the King), Balaam (The Prophet), and the Messenger party, Satan tries this again in Revelation 12 and 13. Another Satanic Trinitarian attempt is made in the personification of Satan, the Antichrist, and the False Prophet. Evil is always attempting to cloak itself in truth and to convince people that it is God. We all know, as in the story of Balaam cooking his own goose, that at the end of all things, Christ spoils Satan's smoke-and-mirror show when he swings his sword and cuts Satan and all his followers off at the neck.

THE PSYCHOLOGY (PERSONAL PAIN & MOTIVE)

A false teacher, or a wolf, is someone who snatches up sheep (Jhn. 10:12), draws disciples away from the gospel (Acts 20:28), opposes the truth (2 Tim. 3:8), and leads people to make a shipwreck of the faith and embrace ungodliness (1 Tim. 1:19-20; 2 Tim. 2:16-17). Both Keith and Balak/Balaam fit the profile that Scripture gives of a false teacher.

However, in considering the psychology of a wolf in sheep's clothing, we must ask ourselves why they are so effective? I mean, it's fairly easy to discern their motives, right? One who lies in wait to kill others is manipulative, murderous in intent, deceptive, and driven by death. Yet even in the reality of it all, the Scripture is very honest with all of us that **all of us** are very prone to becoming false teachers and to give in to those that are. We easily believe them.

But why? Why is it so easy for all of us to give in to that which is false?

The above question may be very easy to answer, but very hard to discern. Though it's easy to just say "that's false" or "that's true" to anything we hear, it's hard to really uncover in ourselves and in others what really drives our "hip-hip-hooray." All our motives for believing one thing and rejecting another lurks under the surface. The reason wolves and false teachers are so very effective at devouring and tricking people into their jaws is that they dress up in sheep's clothing. They hide the truth. They hide in plain sight. They cover up. They conceal things. When we are hiding inside, and covering up our own sin in plain sight, we are particularly susceptible to their honeyed words.

The Bible tells us that shameful hiding is the nature of sin, and as people prone to making mistakes, it's not very hard to see how we can get easily sucked into lies. If we are giving into sin and secrecy inside, chances are we give the enemy a foothold.

But let us not spend too much time on the motives of a false teacher. I think we can all agree to some extent that someone who teaches what is false does not have the best interest of others at heart. Considering that we are all so prone to believing falsely or leading others astray ourselves, let's consider false teaching from a fuller angle. Let's consider what one might look for as a sign that they or someone is giving into false teachings. The germ and the inner psychology of a person buying into false teaching will show forth in symptoms easy to diagnose.

2 Peter 2:1-3, 10-16 is very useful here in helping us understand how to diagnose false teaching:

> But false prophets also arose among the people, just as there will be false teachers among you, who will secretly bring in destructive heresies, even denying the Master who bought them, bringing upon themselves swift destruction. And many will follow their sensuality, and because of them the way of truth will be blasphemed. And in their greed they will exploit you with false words. Their condemnation from long ago is not idle, and their destruction is not asleep. Bold and willful, they do not tremble as they blaspheme the glorious ones, whereas angels, though greater in might and power, do not pronounce a

blasphemous judgment against them before the Lord. But these, like irrational animals, creatures of instinct, born to be caught and destroyed, blaspheming about matters of which they are ignorant, will also be destroyed in their destruction, suffering wrong as the wage for their wrongdoing. They count it pleasure to revel in the daytime. They are blots and blemishes, reveling in their deceptions, while they feast with you. They have eyes full of adultery, insatiable for sin. They entice unsteady souls. They have hearts trained in greed. Accursed children! Forsaking the right way, they have gone astray. They have followed the way of Balaam, the son of Beor, who loved gain from wrongdoing, but was rebuked for his own transgression; a speechless donkey spoke with human voice and restrained the prophet's madness.

There is a lot to be unwrapped in this enormous and weighty set of verses, but I want to sum up Peter's message to one word, ***demeanor***. Demeanor refers to how one carries themselves. Their posture. Tone of Voice. Actions. Works.

Every *root* of a tree produces *fruit*, and though our motives and underlying secrets are like roots that you can't see, anyone can take a look at our fruit and infer some truths about what is going on under the surface. The rotten fruit of a false teacher dances around like a juicy apple, but like any rotten apple, if you just give it a little squeeze a whole mess of junk will spew out telling you that the apple is a phony.

The ***demeanor*** of the false teacher is bold. Willful. They refuse to carry their inner rebellion loudly and proudly in many cases—this makes it too easy to see they are false (we all know loud and proud false teachers). On the contrary, false teachers differ in their approach when compared to antichrists. An antichrist is loud and fully formed in their opinion, whereas false teachers are normally secretive, calculated, well dressed, strategic, contemplative, and greedy in how they get what they want.

Antichrists are the air war. Loud. False teachers come from the sea in submarines. They are deep. They emerge. The text of Peter tells us that they will masquerade as believing truth, and yet they will blaspheme and speak badly about God's believers, angels, and even God himself in the process. Willful hypocrisy.

A false teacher will act and speak out of instinct, not wisdom. Their words will resonate with the way the world works but have nothing to do with the kingdom. Their teachings seem right-side-up and easy to swallow. The kingdom's teachings, on the other hand, are downright upside-down when compared to how we normally think. Real truth requires humility to stomach it.

False prophets aim to give people what they **want** to hear not what they **ought** to hear. They will multiply kisses as the proverbs say. They will flatter. They will entice. They are enticing. Peter says that the eyes of those falling into falsity are full of idolatry and that their appetites cannot stay dormant for long. The tell-tale signs of over-eating, indulging in laziness, slipping away to be alone all the time, and lustful stares, serve as loud evidence that false teaching is grabbing hold.

False teaching is isolating. A person giving into false belief walls themselves off or they gather everyone to themselves. It's an odd type of seclusion that breeds the mob. One-on-one explosion. They speak boldy but only in small groups at first, and off in corners. They begin with speculation and "philosophy" like Keith, and pretty soon they will proclaim they have the answers, calling into question all theology and orthodoxy. Their secrecy will become **loud** once they've mounted enough of an attack. They are sneaky, but they know when to pounce. They are glory seekers. They want the center of attention but they are patient to wait for the stage. They want everyone looking to them as the isolated loner and sole knower of truth.

In 1 Peter, he tells us that absorption with what is untrue makes a person "nearsighted and blind." False teachers will stop seeing. They will become forgetful. And of what? 1 Peter says they forget virtue and the love of the other. They'll forget the real work of truth. Peter says that real knowledge leads to self-control, to steadfastness, to brotherly affection, and finally to love. In all a false teacher's claims of being right, they will live wrong in every fashion.

It's really that simple. The false teacher is driven by an inner 2-year-old that says "look at me." Sadly our society is fashioning false teachers by the millions. We train every child to seek out the center of attention, we tell them only what they want to hear, and we allow them to be the sole authority on what they believe is the truth. On a brighter note, false teachers are getting easier and easier to spot because the majority of our society operates as loud outspoken **antichrists**, or as inward, secretive, manipulative **false prophets.**

43 / COMMUNITY PAIN & MOTIVE

The psychology of sin brings with it a very specific type of community. False communities isolate. They are cultic. They separate, they do not integrate. While isolating, a community that embraces false hope will become louder and louder about what they are against rather than what they are for. They will spend time pointing fingers. Blame is at the heart of their sin, just as in the first sin of Adam and Eve in the Garden of Eden. Communities of false teaching will refuse to take responsibility. They will play the perpetual victim card. They'll never own up to their part in any matter.

They will only speak badly. They will shout venomously about this or that person. Why? Because they are driven by jealousy, covetousness, and competition. Each person in the community wants the first chair. They will despise anyone telling them what to do. Obeying any type of authority is only weakness in their mind. One can only imagine how long a community like this can actually sustain themselves while swimming in a pool of narcissistic insecurity and distrust.

But they stay together.

Today, many false teachers hang together for long periods of time. They unite under a common bond of rebellion. They can stand each other just as long as those beside them refuse to challenge them. They are held together by agreement. Amen. They agree that their community is right. As such, they will begin to define themselves by their own **critique** and **questions.** After all, if all authority is supposedly founded in the false teacher and the false community, the community then has the ability to look at everyone and say, "You are wrong and we're right." This mob-sense of "we're correct" gives off the allure of power, and power is what drives the false teacher. It's not a dictator type power, it's a manipulative power. The Puppeteer. The false teacher knows they are subtly capturing people with their deceptions, and this gives them a sense of control.

While appearing to be bold, this community is full of what Peter calls unsteady souls. They are fearful. In pain. Wounded. Insecure. They pretend to be pit-bulls, but if cornered, they will only whine, lick their wounds, and guard themselves with the shallow yap of a trapped puppy. Insecurity causes the community as a whole to reach for things that give a sense of protection and safety. In the story of Balaam, and in Peter's analysis of Balaam in the previously cited passage, we are told that he did all that he did for the pleasure of "gain in wrongdoing."

Balaam shores up his own personal accounts. He invests in his bank. He wants the money. Safety. Provision. He carries the desire to have more and to be **bigger.** Balaam obsesses over uncertainties rather than what is certain. Out of speculation springs private interpretation. When private pet peeves are applied to Scripture, rampant personal beliefs violate centuries of tradition and the years of those who faithfully followed Christ.

Needless to say, the kingdom of false teaching is quite a bit different than the kingdom of truth. Let's consider how so. In our pondering of the remedy, we can discover some real healing in our own false beliefs and in our response to those in our life who are false teachers.

The remedy to fix false teaching is not just to preach what is true. Yes, there is a lot to be said of the age-old analogy that explains how counterfeiters learn to differentiate between a fake dollar bill and a real one. Agreed, a detective will spend all their time studying the true dollar. In this way, they can always spot a fake. Nonetheless, false teaching doesn't just show up in **beliefs** only but manifests into **actions**. It appears that Scripture highlights more the **demeanor** of those who are false above and beyond the particulars of every false system.

The remedy to bad teaching has to go deeper than words. I'd like to share a few things that we can do to protect ourselves, heal from the influence of false teachers around us, as well as resist becoming false teachers ourselves.

Let's begin with **Preaching Truth, Not Uncertainty** so as to make sure we continue to emphasize truth's importance. Whereas the false teacher loves to create more doubtful questions via speculation, truth teachers, like Jesus, tap into doubts and uncertainties **with questions** in order to expose a person's insecurity and lead them to more confidence. Jesus never sought to derail faith in his teaching, but he sought rather to give people firmer confidence in all that is true.

Preaching is not just a sermon on a mountain meant to transmit principles of belief. It is that, but not only that. Jesus' preaching came in **truth spoken without words.** Peter phrases it this way:

> Live as people who are free, not using your freedom as a cover-up for evil, but living as servants of God ... in your hearts honor Christ the Lord as holy, always being prepared to make a defense to anyone who asks you for a reason for the hope that is in you; yet do it with gentleness and respect (1 Pet. 2:16, 3:15).

These two verses suggest that a truth-telling Christian must live in such a manner of freedom that people actually take notice. True learning happens when it is no longer the teacher who asks the question, but the person observing the teacher.

Though words are important in preaching, we must also remember that even the demons believe that God exists and they shudder. Demons give some credence to the truth, but yet their actions never change. They're bound. They're not free. Liberation from false teaching is realizing that we have the ability to live in certain truth, not just verbalize it.

It's also a comfort and protection to know that we can spot false teachers. We can look not only at their words, but we can consider their fruit. Many subtle false teachings and wrong beliefs show up in continual actions committed over long periods of time. Observing someone over time can convince an observer to stop listening to a person who preaches a continuous anti-gospel via their lifestyle.

False teachers also create false systems. Preaching is not just something that shapes us from a pulpit. It seeps into how ministry is done, how homes are sustained, and how communities are supported. To protect against, and to heal from our own false teachings, we need to evaluate the whole shape of someone's work. It may be that false teaching is getting access in one area, and we can see it in one aspect of a person's life. In looking at the whole of a person's day-to-day rhythms, it becomes clear if something is truly off.

Stemming from the point above, I want to make another. **Slow Fades Require Slower Protection Processes.** I am wholeheartedly convinced that fading into false teaching is often a subtle, manipulative, and slow slide. Since falling prey to false teaching usually takes a while—a slow fade—the gospel requires us to be shrewd. In order to heal, a discerning church or ministry will do the opposite of what Noah did. Noah allowed Keith quick access to a wealth of leadership and influence. Keith took the quick path to destruction. Noah should have recognized the human tendency to misuse power, and therefore should have, for Keith's own benefit, given him a slower process of entrance.

Not only does a more thoughtful and intentional process of overseeing give the people a longer time to assess the person's character and truthfulness, it helps the person as well. I'm convinced that many fall prey to false teaching because they themselves are raised up too fast. They buy into a kingdom that is quick, not patient. They buy into a kingdom that is a hierarchy, not service. They buy into a kingdom that is about me, not we.

Since the Bible clearly tells us that we are "weak souls" and that's what false teaching preys on, we need processes of growth that grow us into strength. The only way a 2-year-old grows into a healthy adult is through an intentional and steady diet of eating, serving, doing chores, and the like.

Let's dovetail into the next point of the above thought. **Isolation Rests in Embrace.** We can end the power grabbing attempts of a false-someone if we call them out of isolation and into the community. Sure, it's quicker to get things done if we are by ourselves. The "we" takes longer. There are more moving pieces. More personalities. More stuff that gets in the way. One thing that the community does challenge above all is love. It exposes one's ability to love or not to love. The litmus test for one who is believing truth is seen in love. One way to prevent false teachers and heal from false teaching is through the **embrace**. Love. Embracing the person, not the teaching and affording them a safe community through which to embrace people themselves.

To help us better understand what embracing is and isn't, let's first consider a time of conflict in Scripture where Euodia and Syntyche in Philippians were in a heavy disagreement. Paul appeals to each woman separately and urges them to live in harmony—literally, to think the same. Paul's use of the Greek phrase "unity of mind," is used more frequently in Philippians than in any other NT book. That's significant. Whereas discussion and disagreement regarding doctrine and character are at times necessary to honor God, that isn't what Paul is talking about here. Paul is talking about the necessity to unite around the gospel in a military-like fashion because our world is in an all-out war against truth.

Paul does not suggest that these two women embrace each other's every way of thinking. He calls them to unity in the essentials. Unity is crucial for bringing healing to the false teacher. Embracing encourages unity in diversity, yet calls all options to accountability in Christ. The **non-negotiables** and hard-and-fast claims of Scripture are essential to helping us preserve truth. Jesus is Lord, for example, is non-negotiable. However, much discussion can still take place over the **negotiable** practices of Scripture that people tend to disagree on—like over what to eat and what not to eat. Fighting for the essential elements of the gospel—faith, hope, and love toward each other and our Savior—helps ensure a strong and right path for us ahead of our differences.

We as believers must take a posture that encourages embrace. It invites the isolated person in even amidst their differences. It allows them to be open, not secretive. It allows them to be heard, and yet not ignored. It calls them to absolute truths but encourages them to sift through their own convictions as long as the essentials of faith are not abandoned. Another helpful perk is that it actually exposes the rebel faster. A room full of openness, truth, and embracing singles out the one naturally trying to divide.

Closeness gives structure to the false teacher. We paint lines on their soccer field (orthodoxy), and then we encourage them to go play freely inside those lines. The false teacher will begin to see how the laws of the game actually make the game freer, and this can be convincing. If it doesn't win them over, they'll leave.

False teaching has to be brought in to the community. All ideas must be weighed by more than just a few outskirt malcontents. There's a higher standard. Scripture tells us that this is where **Flattery Comes to an End With Truth Spoken in Love.** Manipulation, politeness, and fear of false teachers is replaced with confidence in being together. We can stand up to false teaching in one another and in ourselves together. We do what I call Body politics (Mt. 18:17).

When someone falls into false practice or false belief, there's a system of safety that exists in the local church to walk with that person in truth, not flattery. When a person is caught in believing lies at any level, the person can be confronted in love. A platform of safety is there for the offender and the offended to still maintain the embrace and yet confront each other lovingly.

Finally, the rubber hits the road. A gospel-environment is built around well-being, protection, patient growth, embracing, honesty, and accountability, and the goal to all of this is realized as the believing Christian community becomes like Christ. We become like Jesus. We are no longer bound to assess someone on an educational degree, a background, their charisma, or good feelings; we can **Assess Their Character Over and Above Their Competency and Claims.** All false teachers claim to be competent, but the rubber meets the road when someone's pride is challenged with humility. Reality is checked when kindness is faced with rudeness. All truth about a person comes out when suffering meets expectation. The person is revealed for who they truly are in the life of circumstances.

We see in much of Paul's writings that he measures truth amongst people by who they are and by the community they become. We need to define "true" by the type of community that is formed over and above just what is believed. In doing so, we can assess good teaching, and false teachers lose all credibility. Their character simply disqualifies them. Consider Peter's words again in 2 Peter 1:5-9:

> For this very reason, make every effort to supplement your faith with virtue, and virtue with knowledge, and knowledge with self-control, and self-control with steadfastness, and steadfastness with godliness, and godliness with brotherly affection, and brotherly affection with love. For if these qualities are yours and are increasing, they keep you from being ineffective or unfruitful in the knowledge of our Lord Jesus Christ. For whoever lacks these qualities is so nearsighted that he is blind, having forgotten that he was cleansed from his former sins. Therefore, brothers, be all the more diligent to confirm your calling and election, for if you practice these qualities you will never fall. For in this way there will be richly provided for you an entrance into the eternal kingdom of our Lord and Savior Jesus Christ.

Though none of us have arrived, nor will we ever truly embody this verse, notice how Peter measures faith. Growing into true knowledge absolutely leads people to become more aware of the other—love.

To holistically restore, heal, confront, embrace, and to teach the truth to all those caught in false teaching—including ourselves—we absolutely need the gospel remedy. The gospel is not just about believing the right things, it's also about living in a kingdom that operates by a different set of principles. Remember, the Lord Jesus is **the Way**, the Truth, and the Life, and to be true in the truest sense, we have to walk along his way, while listening to his truth, in order to receive the life he promises.

45 / QUESTIONS FOR DISCUSSION

First, contemplate these questions individually and answer in the space provided, and then join together collectively as a group. Here are some Scriptures that can help guide your discussion:

Verses to Consider: *2 Pet. 3:17; Eph. 4:14; Num. 22-24; Phil. 3:18-19; 2 Tim. 4:3-4; 2 Pet. 1:12-21; 2 Pet. 2.*

1. WHAT ITEM OF "OUTWARD APPEARANCE" tends to impress you in others (e.g. degree, job, class, clothing)?

2. What idol is at the root of what wrongly impresses you?

3. How is it that we are so easily sucked into false teaching by what wows, impresses, or surprises us?

. . .

4. Why is it helpful, in considering Balak, Balaam, and the false missionaries, to realize that evil masquerades on this earth through real false leaders, speakers, missionaries, and princes?

5. Think through the portion of this chapter that talks about the "demeanor" of a false teacher. Can you see where you are prone to any of these descriptors, or where you can see these subtly beginning to operate in those closest to you?

6. The Bible tells us that embracing truth will produce in us a calmer, gentler, wiser, and more composed demeanor. Why do you think this is the case?

7. Discuss some of the remedies in protecting against false teaching. How can this help to bring healing to those already duped by wrong ideas, and how can this protect you and your family as you journey through life?

PART 8
MANIPULATIVE MAYHEM

46 / THE CASE STUDY

H e's convincing. His words are juicy. Savory. Encouraging. Flattering. He always has impeccable timing when making the right promises. There's no one quite like Pastor Benjamin.

All those looking at Pastor Benjamin from a distance might describe him as an **opportunist.** Not in a negative sense, but in the best way possible. In every situation, he's able to size up the other person in order to give them exactly what they need. To the few that are close to Pastor Benjamin, they are very aware of his persuasiveness. Deeper still, they are also aware of how his gifts lay very close to manipulating. He tirelessly gives people what they want in order to get what he needs.

His laugh is infectious and his smile endless. He's hopelessly positive; the type of person that may even call the darkest of skies bright yellow just for kicks. Anyone in Benjamin's shoes may have the same outlook if they had his great situation. Most of his church is his family. They are endlessly supportive of him. Not to mention, any newcomer to New Sights Community Church lends their instant trust to Pastor Benjamin because of all his perceived credibility. Who would not follow someone who has all their families' support?

On top of running the church, Pastor Benjamin is President of a global relief organization that brings aid to all those around the world who are caught in times of suffering and crisis. He balances a family of eight, runs three businesses, and still has time to take naps and fish at his private one-acre pond each and every afternoon.

Today Benjamin's role is to teach the Word of God. Pastor Benjamin begins his teaching for the evening with a parable of sorts. He asks for three volunteers to come to the front as he holds high in the air an un-ripened muscadine. He plays it off as a giant grape and begins to explain to the participants that muscadines are wonderfully juicy and delicious when consumed at the proper time. However, to eat a muscadine before it's ripened leaves the most bitter of tastes behind.

He holds up the unripened fruit before a panel of people who all know the bite of a young muscadine all too well. He challenges them, "I'll bet there is not one of you who is brave enough to eat this savory treat."

Long pause.

The participants look at each other with a slight grin.

He echos again, "I'll bet there is not one who will eat this muscadine. You know why? Because you're too afraid of it."

The silence falls again, but this time the participants look at each other as if to ask, "*Are you gonna try it?*"

Getting a bit fed up, Benjamin sets the fruit down and says, "Okay, I guess you all don't want to help me. I guess you're all too afraid."

At the indictment, one of the tallest, strongest, and best-looking participants grabs the fruit, pops it in his mouth, and begins to chew vigorously. His face turns red. He makes hacking noises. He gags. He does all he can just to make sure this thing goes down and doesn't come back up.

Everyone in the congregation lets out a nervous giggle. Everyone can almost taste sour and feel the pain of the young man. Just as the volunteer begins to collect himself Pastor Benjamin says, "You see ... the way you can get anyone to do what you want them to is to appeal to their pride."

Evan sits in the back of the church and hears the words come from Pastor Benjamin. They enrage him. Unlike many of those in the church, Evan knows his own pride all too well, and he knows something deeper about Pastor Benjamin. He knows what Benjamin does in order to use and take advantage of people. Benjamin uses the trick of the muscadine. He entices people's pride to get them to do what he wants. He'd used it on Evan.

Evan had been in one of the darkest hours of his life. No job. No place to live. Struggling to feed his family. Weak. If anything, carrying around nothing but bruised pride. His pride had created his own mess. Having had a disagreement over ethics with a previous employer, he'd been fired from his job and labeled a rebel. The word rebel nonetheless cannot describe Evan. At the core of Evan lies a simple desire for truth. In his search for God, he tends to grow legalistic. His rules define him. His theology overtakes him. Somewhere along the line, he lost his graciousness. Though he knows his limitations, and in fact carries mostly insecurity, he tends to rule over people with his knowledge in the only way he knows how. Pride.

Benjamin saw Evan coming a mile away. Benjamin pulled up close to Evan. He played the friend. Benjamin told Evan every flattering thing he could possibly want to hear. Benjamin made Evan out to be the victim in the whole situation of his life. He implied that all the blame be placed on Evan's previous employer. His words were not encouraging, only flattering. He spoke to Evan's bitterness in order to get him to eat more of the sour fruit.

Evan took what he thought to be savory fruit. His pride bought into the lie.

By falsely praising Evan and validating his actions, Benjamin left Evan in a far more broken place than dealing only with rejection and tenacious rule-abiding. Evan now lives in delusion. Evan struts around with a certain sense of vindication. Benjamin promises him a better future at New Sights Community Church. He sees in Evan a desire to be at the top. To have influence. To lead. He sees how others attempt to stop Evan and how that frustrates Evan. Pastor Benjamin promises to give Evan everything he could ever want or ask for. He promises Evan a muscadine, so to speak. He promises Evan all that's bad for him and nothing that he needs.

It didn't take long before Pastor Benjamin lost interest in Evan's inner struggles. The opportunist had landed the client, hooked him with flattery and manipulation, and now had Evan drinking from his hand. What else did he need? Evan was alone in thinking that Pastor Benjamin offered real promise.

Evan sits more alone than ever on the bench listening to the sermon. Not only did Pastor Benjamin hook his pride, but he had ditched him. It didn't happen right away, but it happened when Evan got too close to Pastor Benjamin. In the process of exposing his own grief, Evan saw a bit too much of Benjamin's "real" side. Benjamin became a bit too exposed, honest, and open. Evan saw deep into the real manipulation underneath the facade of Pastor Benjamin.

Pastor Benjamin's only attempts at a relationship with Evan were to call him into his office in order to ask him to compromise in different areas. The greatest deception requested of him of recent was to ignore the fact that the Pastor's son, Roe, was living in sexual sin with two different women, yet still remaining on staff at the church. Pastor Benjamin used his bait of manipulative power over Evan as leverage to ensure that Roe's sin remained a secret.

Right before the sermon on the muscadine, Evan had had enough with Benjamin's requests of compromise. He had confronted Pastor Benjamin and his son in hopes of breaking the spell that Pastor Benjamin had cast on him.

His confrontation was followed only by mockery from the two Pastors.

"Who is going to believe you, Evan?" mocked Pastor Roe.

"It's our word against yours …" prodded Pastor Benjamin.

47 / THE STORY

What happens next in the story of Evan and Pastor Benjamin does not really matter. The stage of manipulation is set. Suffice it to say, things got legal. What is more important is to discuss the case study of Pastor Benjamin in order to consider how manipulation infects fallen guides and allows those under them to be easily duped. Manipulation is a common disease of sinful rebellion that plagues those already exposed, and those not yet discovered.

The story of Jacob and Esau in Scripture shares with us a similar tale.

Jacob and Esau are the sons of Isaac and Rebekah. They are the first twins mentioned in the Bible. We can only imagine the common bond that exists between twins. Not only are they intensely connected, but they also struggle to be increasingly competitive. With twins, a temptation always exists to differentiate themselves from one another. It's only natural to want to define one's own personhood, yet a good thing can turn cancerous. It's always a difficult balance to maintain a desire for something healthy and yet still not allow it get out of hand, and we know in the story of Jacob and Esau, their competition grew poisonous from within the womb.

Slipping through the birth canal, Esau enters the world first with his brother Jacob literally nipping at his heels. Jacob grasps at his brother trying to pull him back into the womb so that he can come into the world first. His attempt fails. Esau wins the first competition.

Their parents, Isaac and Rebekah, raise Jacob and Esau very differently. Maybe it's a twin thing. Maybe it's just because their personalities are so different. Who knows? All we know is that Jacob is a "quiet man, staying among the tents." He is his mother's favorite in our story. He's domesticated and kept inside. The teacher's pet. Esau, on the other hand, is a "skillful hunter, a man of the open country." He is father's favorite. He's unleashed and allowed to explore and wander.

After hunting in the field one day, Esau returns home to the smell of lentil soup brewing over the fire. His lips pucker. He salivates. He loves Jacob because Jacob cooks so well.

"Can I have some of that soup," he asks the chef?

Jacob is the chef. He's a culinary master. He's a homebody. The artsy type.

"Of course you can," he says.

The interchange is cordial, pleasant, and as to be expected. What comes next is quite shocking.

"Hey Esau," Jacob says again as Esau is leaving the room to get cleaned up, "I'll give you some stew, but I want your birthright in exchange."

The birthright in Jewish culture is everything. It's a special honor that the oldest son possesses. It gives the oldest the right to a double portion of his father's inheritance. Jacob attempts again to be first in the world. He wants to beat Esau. He wants what Esau has.

Like Pastor Benjamin, Jacob is convincing. His words are

juicy. Savory. Encouraging. Flattering. He plans his moment. He shows up with impeccable timing while making the right food in order to get what he wants. He's manipulative.

All those looking at Jacob from a distance might describe him as an **opportunist.** In his situation with Esau, he's able to size him up in order to give him exactly what he thinks he needs. To the few that are close to Jacob, they are very aware of his persuasiveness. Deeper still, they are also aware of how his gifts lay very close to manipulating. He tirelessly gives people what they want in order to get what he needs.

It may seem foolish, but Esau pays the request no thought at all. He says, "Sure." He succumbs to Jacob's manipulation without any discernment. Esau puts his temporary physical hunger over his God-given blessing and he sells his birthright to Jacob (Gen. 25:27-34).

Esau loses everything while thinking he has lost nothing. In the New Testament, Esau's choice to sell his birthright is used as an example of ungodliness. Esau puts his physical desires above spiritual blessings (Heb. 12:15-17). Esau teaches us that what we should do is hold to God's promises above man's so as to secure spiritual blessings. Esau lost his blessing and the New Testament tells us he lost all included in the line of the Messiah (Mal. 1:2-3; Rom. 9:11-14).

Jacob, on the other hand, gains everything. He is remembered today as a member of the Abrahamic covenant. His entrance into that covenant comes through manipulation. Not only did he trick Esau, but he had to coerce his father Isaac to do it. He went to his father with the help of his mother Rebekah, dressed up like the fuzzy Esau, approached his blind father, and stole what was never his to begin with.

Jacob's heist leaves Esau the victim. It draws Rebekah in as the culprit. It deceives Isaac and makes him out to be the fool.

48 / THE PSYCHOLOGY (PERSONAL PAIN & MOTIVE)

For, as I have often told you before and now tell you again even with tears, many live as enemies of the cross of Christ. Their destiny is destruction, their god is their stomach, and their glory is in their shame. Their mind is set on earthly things (Phi. 3:18-19).

There's a difficult balance that we must consider in the story of Jacob and Esau and in the scenario of Pastor Benjamin and Evan. Many leaders and followers fail and continue to fail because they mistake **persuasiveness** with **manipulation.** One serves people, the other uses people. One of them unleashes people to walk in freedom, and the other binds others up more tightly in their own bondages. One hopelessly devotes themselves to the benefit of the other, and the other is cancerous and self-centered.

In the Philippians verse above, Paul targets the motive of manipulation. He says that those who are enemies of the gospel seek to fill their own stomachs and glory in the things that are actually destroying them. In both cases, with Esau and Evan, their smooth operator (Jacob and Benjamin), moved stealthily. To manipulate Esau and Evan they didn't have to really do anything but play to the selfishness, pride, and insecurity already in them. Esau wanted food. Evan wanted power. Esau wanted to be served and Evan wanted people to serve at his orders.

All Jacob and Benjamin did was to learn how to exploit people's weaknesses. They learned how to give people what they wanted while depriving them of what they need. This is what manipulation does. It uses people, it doesn't better people. Jacob and Benjamin were the storied Santa Clauses that came and promised Esau and Evan the world when in reality all that was on the table was the bitter muscadine fruit.

The plot sounds familiar. It's the same tactic Satan used in the Garden of Eden to get Adam and Eve to buy in. He made Adam and Eve discontent. He called God into speculation. He made Adam and Eve feel like they were missing something, and then he swooped down to offer them a life that their "good God" was supposedly keeping from them. All bitterness is born in discontent and it's why the author of Hebrews says that it very easily can grow up and defile many. When discontented people meet people promising them satisfaction, the sickness spreads.

All any manipulator has to do is to play in to someone's pride. All they have to do is stroke someone's belly, feed them what they crave, and praise them for the sin they count as glory. This is how all coercion works. The only catch is that manipulation brings with it slavery.

Persuasiveness is different. It anchors in a different set of truths. Paul continues to write about the root of persuasiveness in Philippians 3:20-21:

> But our citizenship is in heaven. And we eagerly await a Savior from there, the Lord Jesus Christ, who, by the power that enables him to bring everything under his control, will transform our lowly bodies so that they will be like his glorious body.

Persuasiveness refuses to buy into a vision of the future that's as small as a person's appetites. Bottom line, Esau's vision of the good life was too small. Evan's flailing attempts to be on top were too polluted. Each one failed to buy into the deeper truth that we already "have it all." We have citizenship in a kingdom far beyond this life if we'll merely lift our eyes, notice, and believe. Whereas our lowly bodies crave nothing but death in this life, our heavenly and indestructible body awaits. We look forward to a new body that does not hunger. In the kingdom, our new bodies are endowed with the stuff of legend. We possess the power of superheroes.

When compared to a bowl of lentil soup, and Evan's desire to make everything a slave to his view of truth, God's vision of *contentment* reaches far deeper.

The Jacobs and Benjamins of the world fail to realize the same vision of contentment. They live in a world where every resource exists to serve them. They live in a world where being a puppeteer seems to promise power. They love pulling strings. It's protection for them. It's safe. It's fun to mess with people's souls and have no one notice the difference.

Sadly, the manipulator lives in as much bitterness toward God as the manipulated. They are both playing the same game. They are both rejects seeking a crowd who will call them cool. The manipulated eats the fake carrot dangling in front of their face because they hunger for what's false. The manipulator continues to buy into their own delusion that they are master of all. Each snaps at a fake carrot. One promises a real meal. One believes they have a real meal. The reality? Both of them live in torment because neither knows where to get real food.

Our Father tells us how to get the real sustenance. The bread of life. It's found at his banquet in the kingdom.

49 / COMMUNITY PAIN & MOTIVE

Let's contrast the meal found at the table of the manipulative as opposed to the food found on the table of one who persuades:

At the table of the manipulative, the host offers what is unhealthy and calls it nutritious. This game plays out around any number of different scenarios. In Evan's case, he wanted fame, fortune, control, and to make a name for himself. In Esau's case, he wanted comfort, sustenance, his fleshly desires met, and to be entertained. Benjamin and Jacob both laid down tantalizing promises and yummy dishes. They promised it was nutritious. They promised their food would give to Evan and Esau all they wanted and more. Maybe in some manner, they were right. Evan and Esau were hungry for the wrong things, and they went to the wrong meal to meet their needs. Benjamin and Jacob met that need. It was not healthy for them, yet they believed otherwise. Giving people the ability to sin more is never nutritious for any soul.

~

AT THE TABLE of the persuasive, the host provides what is nutritious in a way that tastes good. When eating healthily, creating nutritious, good-tasting food is a challenge. In God's kingdom, love speaks healthy truths to people in savory ways. Love is how we persuade people. Love gives people what they need most for their benefit. What Esau needed was not more comforts, praise, and entertainment; he needed to learn to value his brother and God's gifts. Evan didn't need to be put in charge; he needed to be made to serve. Evan needed training. He needed humility. He needed to take the back seat.

For the Evans and the Esaus of the world, persuasiveness is never the easy thing. Their body wants junk food, and it's the responsibility of the loving persuader to teach them that the body is really seeking nutrition. For the Jacobs and the Benjamins of the world, persuasiveness is equally difficult. They are forced to consider what someone else may need. They are forced to assess the situation from how it can benefit the other. For the Jacobs and the Benjamins, this may mean that their service may cost them something. To be persuasive always requires sacrifice.

AT THE MANIPULATOR'S table is the endless promise that there is a seat in the head chair but there is in reality never a chair. The manipulator always appeals to pride by dangling something that doesn't exist. They offer the head place though they always take the spot themselves. They occupy the center of attention. Everything revolves around their judgment, their decisions, and their move.

They offer the listener anything they want. They offer hopes and dreams and smoke and mirrors. It's not about wants, it's about the desires of the one in power. Manipulators always have agendas. It's never to give the person what they want, though giving people what they want for a time serves as great bait.

Manipulators parade everyone to the head of the table, make them feel important, and give them a little flattery and taste of what the high life is like, but when the lights come on, there's no chair. It's all a game.

AT THE TABLE **of the persuasive** is the truth that sitting in the chair can only lead to destruction unless the person sitting there has first sat in the last seat. It's kingdom. Jesus said that we must all desire the last chair. The chair of service. The lowly place. The humble place. Only then can we truly occupy the seat we may want. Choosing humility postures a person to see the world rightly. They see themselves as lowly. If after and through service they are given the chair at the head of the table, they will continue posturing themselves as lowly. There's no greater way to see one's self than being one of low esteem if we want to be effective at meeting the needs of a needy world. We need to know that we too are needy.

For the manipulative, the client always considers themselves deserving, but never needy. In persuasion, the client considers themselves always needy and thankful when given all they don't deserve. It's a different posture.

AT THE TABLE **of the manipulative** are silent guests that sit and watch while the host eats his/her meal. In the case of Benjamin, he had smoked-screened his own family. He'd intimidated them into silence. The only way to stay close to him was to allow him to be the protector. His safety was coercive. And for those that think the power of suggestion, possibility, and magic will not work on them, consider the powers at work in our world and how easily they make us cower. Manipulation is the power of Hitler. He plays the gentlemen card and only at the end reveals his tricks.

. . .

At the table of persuasion is a host of vibrant guests all eating and sharing conversation. This is huge. Persuasive people do not make people afraid to share openly. People are not walking around concerned with what might be used against them as leverage. Guests don't worry about how the host may wield information about them behind closed doors in order to get what they want. At the table of persuasion, there's unity in diversity. People can share openly what they feel. They can voice concern, celebration, desire, and want, and still be called into more when their desires are far too slim. It keeps Jacobs from festering in secrecy. It keeps Evans from boiling in entitlement. It prevents Pastor Benjamins from exploiting everyone.

A different kind of community is formed. It's the difference between the banquet of Nebuchadnezzar and Esther. Nebuchadnezzar's table and feasts were manipulative. Daniel knew it. That's why he refused to eat. Nebuchadnezzar brought everyone under his spell at his feasts. He entertained the people's flesh with sex, drink, and rock 'n' roll, and only demanded one thing—that they worship him. When people failed to bow to Nebuchadnezzar, he tried to have them killed.

Esther's feast, on the other hand, was persuasive. She found out that the evil overlord Hamaan was going to kill her people, so she prepared a meal for Hamaan and the King. She made them feel at home. She brought them under a spell of comfort, entertainment, and honesty. When given the chance in the meal to wield her power, she didn't use it for her own worship. The king asked her to tell him anything she wanted, and he would do it, and she thought only of the other. In essence, her words were, "Let God's people go."

Creating a table of **persuasion** and not one of **manipulation** is the gospel. Jesus is very clear in all his banquet analogies that people are to be **invited** to come to his feasts and never **coerced** or forced. Manipulation takes advantage of people by exploiting them, but Jesus' call to repentance and to a life lived in humility is anything but. He never exploits us to use us, he meets our needs to such a full extent that we desire to do nothing but generously volunteer out of our own choice to be used by him.

The Bible teaches us about slavery in the good sense and in the bad. Slavery to sin imprisons. Slavery to righteousness frees. Slavery to Jesus is freeing. The gospel remedy that can deeply heal people who are manipulators, or who are easily manipulated, comes in two truths but unfolds in many applications. The truth that heals both parties is **grace** and **mercy**.

Grace is receiving gifts that are underserved. Mercy is being freely spared from punishments warranted. The gospel does both. Jesus gives us his life and kingdom citizenship. It's undeserved. He withholds from us the wrath and anger due to a servant who has murdered, robbed, and enslaved his family. His mercy holds back our warranted punishments.

The reason that grace and mercy are healing to the manipulator and the manipulated is that the same motive drives both sins, **bitterness.** The manipulator thinks themselves entitled to more, and so they make everything and everyone their servant. The manipulated walk around in discontent and anger at God for what they feel they should have, and yet do not get. They are easy prey for anyone who strokes their pride or promises them what they feel they deserve.

The two simple truths of grace and mercy should transform how we live at every level. We should strive to form paradigms for ministry that make such nutrition desirable. We should live in a manner that makes the servant seat the most desired seat. We should love our wives and husbands in such a manner that makes them more lovable and respectable, and us less noticed. We should call out the idols in each other when we see them. It's an embarrassment that's sometimes necessary. It's an embarrassment that's helpful. It's an embarrassment that saves lives.

Only in being revealed in our worst moments can we truly see the true brilliance of grace and mercy. If manipulators and the manipulated are left to control and desire death without borders, grace and mercy fail to make sense.

To grow people in grace and mercy takes more than mere sermons. It takes exposure. It takes a willing reveal. It requires an overhaul to environments. It requires an overhaul of how we speak. It requires an overhaul in marketing, publicity, and what we put forth as "the good life." To build up people in their knowledge and expression of grace and mercy, servant structures have to be put in place. To be great is to be small. To be full is to be empty. To be blessed is to mourn. To be joyful, as the Beatitudes say, is to be deprived of worldly comforts and given the gospel.

Grasping at heels and climbing ladders has to become out of place, not commonplace.

Capitalism. Business. Church. Education. Government. All of these environments seem to work tirelessly to promote a vision of the good life that is happiest at the top, not the bottom. Kinda' curious isn't it? It's altogether tragic because in God's kingdom, to reach the top, means we need to swim toward the bottom. Incarnation. Jesus modeled for us what it was for God to become flesh.

News headline: ***"Rich King becomes a peasant. An all-glorious perfect Savior becomes a suffering servant."***

Jesus' way of life calls out to all manipulators and says to put yourself in a place where you think about others for kingdom gain. Jesus' way of life calls out to all those manipulated and says, "I came to give you life … **life more abundant.**" To each person, Jesus makes a better promise. He promises a real chair at the table. He promises lively conversation and helpful confrontation. He promises food which everyone can enjoy. He invites.

You're invited.

51 / QUESTIONS FOR DISCUSSION

First, contemplate these questions individually and answer in the space provided, and then join together collectively as a group. Here are some Scriptures that can help guide your discussion:

1. In what ways are you specifically susceptible to manipulation?

2. What tools of wisdom do you use in order to determine whether something is persuasive, biblical, or glorifying to God in any given situation? What tools does Scripture tell us to use?

3. Discuss the analogy of the "Table" used when talking about communities of manipulation or persuasion. How can you practically build up your table, your family, and your home into becoming an environment where openness and right reasoning thrives?

. . .

4. What are some simple steps we can take to weigh the different options presented to us before going "all in?"

5. Satan often appeals to our entitlement and pride to get us to do something, whereas Jesus usually leads us down a humble and often times less visible road toward his ends. How might God be asking you to follow him today down paths that are more humble? How might your pride be leading your life more than you'd care to admit?

6. How can we posture ourselves day to day to make the gospel more inviting to people?

7. Is there any bitterness in your life that is causing you to manipulate others or be easily manipulated by others?

8. When Jesus says that "abundant life" will be one filled with "much suffering," how does this challenge your way of seeing "the good life?"

9. How are you building into your family, home, and church servant structures that help others embrace a life of loving their neighbors in the manner of Jesus?

PART 9
MAN BEHIND THE MASK

THE CASE STUDY

When someone doesn't seem right it's because they often aren't. This describes Pastor Warren and Grace Chapel in Dixon, TN.

Grace Chapel is a unique church for the south. As we'll see, its uniqueness will play out in many forms. Let's call form one, Grace 1.0. Pastor Warren (he'll shortly enter as the main character) is a unique kind of leader. How so, you ask? Well, let's begin by describing the current context in which Pastor Warren finds himself.

In the church world of the South, congregations are known more by skin color than by denomination or belief. Black. White. The South is really black and white. In or out. Accepted or not. The funny thing, however, is the racial pollution skims only the surface of the real issues. Under the shimmering waves lies a deep undercurrent of gray. Social cues are prized above all. Every comment is laden with expectation and nuance. Every tradition carries with it an intention. If you don't know how to read the signals, you're lost. Ostracized. You won't fit in.

Dixon is a place that follows social norms that are all too often reflective of the culture that formed prior to civil rights. It's difficult to find people that actually think like Jesus. Inclusive. All peoples. All nations. It's easy to find many preachers screaming the good news loudly and proudly but when it comes down to how the gospel actually embraces "the other," I'm not so sure many people feel the good news of the gospel on the streets of this Tennessee town.

Grace Chapel is of a particularly different kind of DNA. On one hand, they actually embrace the outcast position. The rebel. The different. Amongst all the churches in the South, they house a congregation that represents over thirteen nations. The congregation is not primarily comprised of black and white alone, but it is rather colorful. It's filled with differing personalities. Languages. Cultural backgrounds. Denominational differences. I could go on.

Grace's church structure is labeled the rebel. Its current Pastor, everyone calls him Cartwright, is a deviant. In all actuality, Grace and Cartwright strive to represent the Kingdom of God. In the eyes of Jesus, seeing life in only black and white is abnormal. Limited. Bigoted. Small. Colorful is what is normal to our Savior. He's robust. Big. He's a God of embracing.

What also makes Grace abnormal is that it is young. It's a church plant. Only a year old. The foundational planting team, though made up of black and white thinkers, somehow now have the "whole world" dropped in their lap. Though they still possess their vanilla way of approaching everything, they somehow discover that God has brought the nations to them. They embrace those that are different, but they still struggle to understand them. They limp along trying not to be exclusive, but they still embrace the status quo. The religion of their choice still naturally fits into tidy little cultural holes. They are trying to think more kingdom, but like many of us, still, don't have a clue what that looks like.

Enter Pastor Warren.

Pastor Warren lives in the East Indies. Originally from the South, but twenty years removed as a missionary church planter and educator, Pastor Warren definitely thinks and acts more naturally in "kingdom." His view and understanding of God are big. Diverse. Unified.

Pastor Warren is what some may also call a Genius. He's theological. Brilliant. A Master-craftsman. Creative. Colorful. Multicultural. Traveled. Oh, and did I say a Genius? Upon entering into the mix of Grace Chapel as a visitor, it takes mere seconds for the current leader of the budding congregation—Pastor Cartwright—to recognize his inability to lead such a diverse group of people.

Hats off to Cartwright. His initial response to Pastor Warren is humility. He admits his limitations and lack of ability in how to lead the specific dynamics of Grace. He lacks the ability to understand the nations in his congregation. At least for now. He's a freshwater fish in a deep blue ocean. He embraces that he's out of his league.

Over the following six months he rushes to Pastor Warren for help. His pleas go so far as to make a request of Pastor Warren to consider moving to Dixon in order to lead Grace. Pastor Warren, rather than seeking a job as a "senior" leader, whatever that means, cuts through the red tape and envisions something different. He comes to Cartwright and says, "Let's lead this together."

And why not? It's a brilliantly explosive idea. Heck. It's more biblical. It has the instant possibility to go extremely bad, or extremely good. Despite what one might think upon first glance—namely that this is a HORRIBLE idea—Cartwright and Warren have the ability to run like a well-oiled machine if they might only think in terms of **cars**.

Cartwright is the brakes. Warren is the gas. Both are needed to successfully and safely guide a car, particularly when the vehicle is venturing into new and uncharted territory. The perfect balance of caution and small-mindedness, mixed with the all too often colorful recklessness of those who jump in head first, provides the perfect balance for innovation. Creativity. What Grace needs is to have both left and right brains. Its how the kingdom of God works, really. It takes the Body.

Together Cartwright and Warren need to help others embrace the culture at hand and all its dynamics—both good and bad. However, they also have the responsibility from God to welcome God's sovereign plan to "do a new thing" (actually, more like a very old thing). To think in ways conducive to "The Kingdom of God," Grace, along with all Christians, need a balance of both people who are shrewd and innocent with a tendency toward being too cautious and safe, and those who are forceful trailblazers who often live out a "Big-God" theology, and yet sometimes have a tendency toward a lack of discernment and wisdom.

Remember when I mentioned Grace 1.0? Well, now enters Grace 2.0! Grace 1.0 was a beta test gone wrong. Despite good intentions, the original planting members somehow planted a church that miraculously drew together the nations but did very little to learn how to include, embrace, or grow in Christ alongside them. Grace 1.0 had no idea how to achieve an "us." It had always been an "us against them."

Grace 2.0 ushered in a day that gave Pastor Warren more say in things. Pastor Warren, not being a shy person, spoke loudly, proudly, boldly, and swiftly. Pastor Warren began moving so quickly in an altogether opposite direction that one started to wonder if Cartwright was in the car any longer as a fellow driver, or if Pastor Warren had merely left him in his skids.

Nonetheless, the church grew and grew and grew. Leaps and bounds. Nations were added. Deep and rich meals were assembled. Eating together and doing life with one another became the DNA of Grace 2.0. Creativity started to emerge. The people were beginning to speak and have a voice. People were becoming a we. The once vanilla church was starting to taste like Neapolitan ice cream.

Meanwhile, a different kind of grey brewed beneath the surface of Pastor Warren.

People at Grace started to sense something was off. Pastor Warren was inspiring, but distant. Secretive even. He turned Genius into calculation and manipulation. Cartwright kept pushing the brakes as hard as he could, but it seemed Pastor Warren had snipped the cables. Cartwright's attempts to help failed. Cartwright began despising Warren. Warren started blaming Cartwright for all things gone wrong.

It doesn't take a genius to see the writing on the wall, however, everyone was surprised by exactly how the anvil fell.

Grace, though appearing to be advancing smoothly, became a cesspool of secrecy and manipulation. Cartwright recruited and preserved his side of things out of growing distrust for Pastor Warren, and Pastor Warren did the same on his end. Two sides developed. One side advanced, while the other side was silenced. Pastor Warren began to compete, not pastor. Cartwright started to give up and lose courage.

What had been Grace 2.0, turned into Grace 3.0. It no longer reflected where Cartwright had started it, and it no longer reflected a DNA of "life together." It was Pastor Warren's church now.

That is until the list came out.

A website named *Olivia's Closet* was hacked. The website was built solely around the idea of giving married men a place to have affairs in secrecy. When hackers got ahold of the database, they exposed everyone on it. Lists went out into every town. Pastor Warren's name topped the list.

Scandal. Immorality. Adultery. Lies brought into the light. Pastor Warren was immediately asked to step down from any kind of leadership while an investigation took place. Sadly, his exploits were not confined to *Olivia's Closet*, but his perversion extended into emails, hook-up sites, rampant pornography use, Craigslist, prostitution, and more.

Cartwright led the team to help investigate Pastor Warren's secrets with the intent to help restore Pastor Warren and his family.

I WISH I could say the story has a happy ending. It does not. It ends pretty much like many of these situations do, but worse. At first, Pastor Warren seemed repentant, but still, something felt off. Though the current team of overseers asked him to bring his sin before the congregation for healing and forgiveness, Warren only obliged half-heartedly through emails and letters. In presence, he all but disappeared. His words sounded contrite and he isolated. He didn't come to church. He hid behind the emails.

Grace 4.0 began. Not only did Cartwright lead the dwindling church back to where they had once been, they actually succeeded at becoming more vanilla than before. Pendulums have a tendency to always swing to extremes and swing they did. Never to balance. Soon the nations left. Quickly the same cultural norm and bigotry that existed before set in as had been previous. Even worse, Pastor Warren began showing his true colors. Wolf colors. He began siphoning off members of Grace. He started a new church.

Israel went through its share of 1.0, 2.0, 3.0, 4.0 and more. In the time of the judges, leaders changed hands more often than hairstyles. Judges and rulers would come in and honor God. Things went good. Judges would die or be usurped by those that didn't honor God. Things went bad. Mostly bad.

In fact, things went so bad, theologians today coin what happened during that time as the *Judges Cycle*. The cycle refers to a repetitive style of leadership and Israel's sin. Israel would be actively serving the Lord, only to be drawn into sin and idolatry by a new leader. As a result, they would become slaves, they would cry out to the Lord, and God would mercifully raise up a Judge to set to deliver them. Israel would once again begin serving God again. The cycle repeated itself over and over and over again.

In the table below you can see the spiritual toll that this cycle took on the people through a constant cycle of bondage, deliverance, and rest.

Enemy	Years of Bondage	Judge	Deliverance and Rest	Scripture
Mesopotamia	8	Othniel	40	3:7-11
Moab	18	Ehud	80	3:12-31
Canaan	20	Deborah	40	4:1-5:31
Midian	7	Gideon	40	6:1-8:28
Ammon	18	Jephthah	6	10:6-12:7
Philistia	40	Samson	20	13:1-16:31

In the midst of all this chaos, we arrive at Judges 13:1. The passages tell us, "and the people of Israel again did what was evil in the sight of the Lord, so the Lord gave them into the hand of the Philistines for forty years." Time after time Israel kept landing in bondage, and time and time again God continued raising up new leaders. Let's call it Judges 10.0.

THE LORD COMES to a man in the tribe of Zorah whose name is Manoah. He comes specifically to Manoah's wife in the form of an angel (Judg. 13:2-3). Manoah's wife at this time is barren. The angel promises to her that God will indeed bless them with a son, and the angel lays out some very specific guidelines that this boy must follow (Judg. 13:4-5).

He tells her that he is to drink no wine, touch nothing unclean or dead, refrain from shaving, and to be separated and set apart of God's purposes. He is to be a Nazarite. In the same manner as the Levites who were separated from the Jews as ministers to serve in the sanctuary (Num. 3:12-13), to live holy lives (Lev. 21:6), and to abstain from alcohol (Lev. 10), Samson is called to holiness of the highest regard.

The reason that such a degree of holiness is demanded of the boy is made clear by the angel. Manoah's son is to "***begin*** to save Israel from the hand of the Philistines." This boy, Samson, is tasked for a holy errand. The angel flits away into the air as quickly as he came, and sure enough, the birth of Samson follows.

The Scripture tell us that from an early age the spirit of the Lord began to "stir" young Samson. The word used for "stir" in the Hebrew is *pä·am'*. Every time this word *pä·am'* is used in the Old Testament it refers to trouble. The spirit of God moved upon Samson with great conviction and refinement as the scriptures tells us. It can be assumed that Samson developed a deep conviction of faith and a deep heart for God's people through this time.

Many know the story of Samson's tragic life and fall into countless temptations, so it is not important to recount every detail for our purposes here. It is important however to recognize that Samson's life, as we see in the first part of Judges 13, is a life of great promise and intention by God.

God's work through Samson is meant to completely free Israel from the Philistines. In Judges 14, we are told that Samson goes to a town called Timnah and is drawn to a beautiful woman; a daughter of one of the Philistines. His response to her beauty is to run back home and tell his parents. One can only imagine what Samson's mother and father must have felt when Samson came back and said of their enemy, "get her for me, for she is right in my eyes." The account tells us "that his father and mother did not know **it was from the Lord**, for he was seeking an opportunity against the Philistines (Jug. 14:4)." Though Samson's seemingly lustful eyes are hastily on the prowl, God works behind the scenes doing something in Samson's life despite his sins.

His family and he left to go down to Timnah to take up the fair Philistine woman, and along the road, they encounter a lion. It came toward them in what we can only assume to be an intimidating posture. Samson attacks the lion and tears it limb from limb. Maybe he acts as he did to show off, or maybe to protect his parents who were with him. But the text tells us that he did not tell his parents, so most likely he was off by himself doing some exploring on their journey, and like a little boy, did more to destroy the animal than necessary simply to build pride in his heart and in his own strength. Whatever the reason, we are told that **"*the Spirit of the Lord rushed upon him***, and although he had nothing in his hand, he tore the lion in pieces as one tears a young goat."

We're told the above incident results from God's Spirit coming upon Samson. We are later told the same thing when Samson tries to exploit the event with the lion through a riddle told to the woman's companions from the Philistine camp—a riddle told with the intention of humiliating them.

His riddle originates around Samson's return back to Timnah to marry the woman. Samson finds the carcass of his kill, and at home in the rotting flesh are bees. Defying God's mandate that he should not touch anything dead or unclean, Samson reaches in, scoops up some honey and eats. The riddle he tells to the thirty Philistines accompanying his fair maiden is: "Out of the eater came something to eat, and out of the strong came something sweet."

The men are bewildered. Four days go by, and they still cannot solve the meaning. This little game that Samson plays with his new bride's friends and family deeply upsets her and she manipulates Samson into telling her the secret. After doing so, she spills the beans to her friends, who in turn come to Samson with the answer.

Samson is furious. He's been betrayed. His game is over. The fun is gone. He can no longer laugh and mock the Philistines in their stupidity and bewilderment. He loses the bet. What he loses in the wager is thirty linen garments and changes of clothes. Samson, being poor and owning the men such high price, can't afford such a bounty, so he goes down into the Philistine town of Ashkelon and kills thirty men and takes their garments to pay off his debt to the men holding the answer to the riddle.

To say the least, this mass murder is nothing short of a horrible tale of disobedience, temper, and violence, but in Judges

14:19, as Samson goes down to destroy the men in Ashkelon, we are once again told that it happened because *"**the Spirit of the Lord rushed upon him** ..."* Samson seems in some manner to learn from this experience because in Judges 15:3, when the Father of his wife withholds her from him and offers his wife's sister instead, Samson vows payback once again on the Philistines, but he says "**this time** *I shall be innocent in regard to the Philistines*, when I do them harm."

Samson, still bitter, rebellious, and conniving, reveals to us the way in which he defines the word "innocence" in the matter. In Judges 15:4-5, "Samson went and caught 300 foxes and took torches. And he turned them tail to tail and put a torch between each pair of tails. And when he had set fire to the torches, he let the foxes go into the standing grain of the Philistines and set fire to the stacked grain and the standing grain, as well as the olive orchards." Samson's actions prove so destructive that the Philistines go to Timnah, kill his wife and father-in-law by burning them alive, and then set up camp in Judah to make war on the tribe of Judah—which the name Judah literally means "the Praise of God." Samson's actions cause warring against those who stand for the praise of the Almighty.

The problem vexes all those in Judah to such a degree that they come to bind Samson with ropes so that the Philistines can come and kill him themselves. But yet again, in Judges 15:14-16 we read, "... ***then the Spirit of the Lord rushed upon him***, and the ropes that were on his arms became as flax that has caught fire, and his bonds melted off his hands. And he found a fresh jawbone of a donkey, and put out his hand and took it, and with it, he struck 1,000 men."

By this point, we have to ask ourselves some questions about this colorful character Samson. Is he faithful and a believer in God as the Bible seems to imply, or a vicious Viking roaming around looking for spoils, sex, and blood? The question may appear easy to answer, but there's constant tension in Samson's life between his sin and what *the spirit of the Lord* is accomplishing through him despite his sin.

In the closing seasons of Samson's life, I think we learn a little about the truth to this man's tragedy. Let's consider two final examples.

First, let's consider the night Samson goes to sleep with a prostitute in Gaza; only to be set up for an ambush by the Gazites. The Scripture tells us that as his enemies lay in wait, he waits for them. Seeking to thwart them, he stays in hiding until midnight to sneak out. Instead of killing them straight away, he takes hold of the doors of the gate of the city and the two posts, and pulls them up, bar and all, and puts them on his shoulders and carries them to the top of the hill that is in front of Hebron (Judges 16:3). One might think this to be an odd way to gain victory over one's enemies, especially when Samson's normal code of conduct is just to swing things and kill people.

Samson's wielding of the gates is a faint whisper of his somewhat dormant faith. He is actively remembering the promise made to Abraham. God came to Abraham in Genesis 22:17 and said, "I will surely bless you, and I will surely multiply your offspring as the stars of heaven and as the sand that is on the seashore. ***And your offspring shall possess the gate of his enemies*** (Gen. 22:17) ..." Samson, in the best way he knows how, acts on promise. He knows of God's commitment to his people and he's been trained in the ways of the Nazarite and the Levite. He knows the strength and call on his life despite his constant failure to live in line with that.

Finally, comes the most famous Samson story of all. Delilah. She tricks him into divulging the source of his supernatural strength. His hair. His hair is cut by his enemies and his strength leaves. He's imprisoned, his eyes are gouged out by the Philistines, and he's made a spectacle to be mocked at their parties. In being stripped of all things, he utters these words, "O Lord God, please remember me and please strengthen me only this once, O God, that I may be avenged on the Philistines for my two eyes." He pushes the pillars holding up the house where all the Philistines are celebrating. The structure collapses, and all 3,000 men and women who looked on "while Samson entertained them," were killed along with Samson himself. Only then does our text specifically name Samson as a Judge in Israel in Judges 16:31.

We have the end of Samson. We have the end of the Philistines. We have the beginning of Samson's title as Judge. The one who eats unclean things (honey from a dead body) (Judg. 14:8), sleeps with prostitutes (Judg. 16:1), acts in anger and vengeance on a host of occasions, and cuts his Nazeritic hair (Judg. 16:17)—only after continually telling lies to Delilah about the source of his true power (Judg. 16:1-22)—lies dead on the floor with Scripture naming him in the highest honor. The spirit of God had left him when his hair was cut (Judg. 16:20), but his last words were a prayer for God's justice.

So what's the answer? Is Samson a man of rebellion or a man of faith? The story seems to imply both. Though holding loosely to God's promises, Samson's divided desires seemed to endlessly get him in trouble. Graciously, and almost unbelievably, however, God's spirit still filled Samson, authenticated him as a Judge of Israel, and accomplished God's purposes in and through him to *begin his deliverance of his people from the hands of the Philistines.*

54 / THE PSYCHOLOGY (PERSONAL PAIN & MOTIVE)

It's pretty obvious to look at the case study of Pastor Warren and Cartwright and say, "I know what went wrong." It's pretty easy to look at Samson and come up with some simple principles as to why Samson's journey is forever remembered as a tragedy. There's nothing terribly profound that I can say here that any of you as readers might not already notice, but let me draw your attention to a few principles that tie together the demise of both characters in our Case Study and our Story from Scripture.

First and foremost, I think we all take for granted the destructive power of **divided passions** dwelling within each us. In Pastor Warren's case, there dwelt inside him an intense desire to include everyone and bring the good news of the gospel to the whole world. It's a beautiful vision. Nonetheless, it's so easy for beauty to be twisted. At the hands of adultery and the female form, his insatiable search for the beautiful landed him in a masquerade of vice over virtue.

In and of itself, the search for beauty is central to each and every one of us. It's a passion. It's what makes us human. Johnathan Edward's believed that "beauty is more central and more pervasive than in any other text in the history of Christian theology."[1] Edwards argued that God's ravishing beauty is the first and most important thing one can say of God. "God is God, and distinguished from all other beings, and exalted above them, chiefly by his divine beauty." Therefore all of nature functions as a school of desire—teaching humans how to see God's glory. We taste things that were once dull but are now made alive (Calvin's idea of sweetness or *suavitas*) —a sixth sense if you will.

There's a crux to every human sin. It's a misunderstanding of beauty. **Divided passions.** On one hand, we have Jesus positively defining his death and resurrection as his *passion*. In Acts 1:3 the whole event of Jesus' greatest horror and victory is called ***the passion***. Yet, on the other hand, in James 4:1-4 we have James writing: "What causes quarrels and what causes fights among you? Is it not this, that your **passions** are at war within you? You desire and do not have, so you murder. You covet and cannot obtain, so you fight and quarrel. You do not have, because you do not ask. You ask and do not receive, because you ask wrongly, to spend it on your **passions**. *You adulterous people!* Do you not know that friendship with the world is enmity with God?" The word for passion used in the Greek in both instances is the same word. Scripture affirms our passion in one respect and warns against it in other. The dichotomy is what Scripture would refer to as being double minded. We cannot have both what we want and what God wants. Either our passion is aimed at serving the beauty of God, or it's not. To lend our attention to any lesser beauty than that of Christ is idolatry and adultery. Double-minded passion is the sin of Pastor Warren and Samson, and I would even say of Cartwright. Though Pastor Warren and Samson's sins were more visible, Cartwright's desires and passions for control, and to bring all people into "one way of being and doing things," is equally twisted. In both instances, they prize their own version of beauty over God's definition of beauty.

Secondly, in both scenarios, each character is very cavalier in **taking liberty with the Holy.** Samson spit on the Nazarite vow, touched dead things, and lived a life that was compromised rather than set apart. Pastor Warren and Cartwright did the same thing, but they took liberties with the greatest and holiest thing—next to God's nature that is. They messed with Christ's Bride. The Church.

When we handle people with an adulterous hand, a lustful eye, or a murderous swing of a jawbone, it's a blatant act of hate toward God's kids and a slight against God. What's even worse is that there are more subtle rebellions operating in the gray just beneath the ocean's swells. Believing that we can use God's family to advance our aims, to accomplish our goals, to press toward our image, or exalt our name, is much more subtle, but equally offensive. We're taking liberty with God's Bride. We're using his Bride for our trophy case. We're using God's wife for our advancement. We're sacrificing love and "one another" for selfish gains and payoffs. We're leaving aside the clear mandates of God and inventing our own rules so that the church stays as vanilla, confined, bigoted, small-minded, and small-godded as us.

Thirdly, in each scenario, I think it's telling how easy it is to **hide behind theology to create an ideology,** and vice-versa. Let me explain.

Everything is theology. Theology is simply the study of God, or "what is supreme." Even those claiming that there is no god have a theology. One's supreme rhyme and reason may attempt to end with them, or with their science, rather than in God himself, but they claim something ultimate nonetheless. They claim an authority just like anyone else. Any claim of "supreme" results in a manufactured life lived in accordance with those beliefs. People deifying their own judgments on divine become the supremacy, and if no supremacy exists beyond one's own mind, then we can easily think that we can make or not make rules for existence. In pitting ourselves as supreme, it becomes logical to say "You can't question me." Our mantra thus turns our utopia into a judgment stick that is wielded to kill off anyone who doesn't agree with us. **A theology based around one's own assumptions results in extremism, extermination, and extinction.**

We see how ideologies resulting from bad theologies emerge all over our world at various levels. Ultimately, at the end of the day, everyone's screaming, "if you don't agree with me, then you're wrong. If you try to inflict 'your thing' on me, then you'll pay for it." This is the culture of sin. It breeds a world of vengeance, hatred, envy, and self-promotion.

Everyone is walking around with their own vision of the good life, and they will achieve their ends by whatever means possible as long as their desires are satisfied. For Pastor Warren, it was manipulation and a sexual hand. For Cartwright, it was a life lived with so many parameters that only someone who looked like him could measure up. For Samson, his good life was one God created for him, but Samson decided to get it through murder, whoring, anger, and trickery. He had the right theology, but the wrong way to go about it.

On the same token, the whole process works in reverse as well. Let's take Samson for instance. He had an ideology of the "good life" lodged in his mind. If you were to ask him, he probably would have told you that the meaning of life is to be **comfortable**. His whole life aimed at this end. His wants were to be satisfied at every point and in his timing. It morphed his theology into something a Christian would hardly recognize. Rather than claiming Abraham's promise as one of blessing for all nations, Samson turned it into a power struggle. In some fashion, he used God's promise to tear down the gates of enemy cities in his own warped version of kingship. Our King in heaven goes about ending power struggles in a manner altogether different from Samson.

He does it in Jesus.

Christ dies on our behalf for his glory and our best interest. Christ, in turn, becomes victorious over all powers in rising again.

Samson believed his life to be special. Is this true? Yes. Of course. Every life is special, but Samson took it to a place of entitlement. His ideology was "I'm special" and his conclusive theology was that "everyone in the universe should thus serve and bow to me." Again, the right things are going on in his head and heart but wrong applications are made from wrong conclusions, which results in everyone getting hurt.

---

[1] Farley, E. *Faith and Beauty: A Theological Aesthetic* (Burlington, VT: Ashgate, 2001), p. 43.

55 / COMMUNITY PAIN & MOTIVE

Samson-like sins hurt us, those who follow us, and ultimately those who form communities that are malnourished and deformed around us. For Samson, everyone lived around a loose cannon. They were afraid of him. He was intimidating. When he wanted to marry a woman and his parents said "not a good idea," the Scripture tells us that they still went with Samson. Why? Fear.

For those in the church serving under leadership that **takes liberty with the holy**, people are treated like commodities, not treasures. People are used. Unfortunately, the local church in many parts of the world has become a machine that eats people, spits them out, and turns to the next entrée. Sad.

Communities are precious and set apart before God, and in his kingdom, and even in our day, certain people claim their race, their sexual orientation, their voice, and their perspective to be most valid. In doing so, they hit communities with their agenda sticks rather than truly caring for people. They take liberty with the holy. They use their own bodies in ways they deem fit. They treat others how they themselves see fit, not how God would have them treated, and it forms a community similar to the manner of

Samson. They take what they want when they want. And you must not dare question them, or they'll come after you on a killing spree.

I think the common denominator in Pastor Warren's case and in the story Samson is to see that taking liberties with the holy (God's people and ways) leads toward unholiness. It's no surprise that Samson or Pastor Warren got caught up in sex and perversion. Sexual abuse is the ultimate end of taking liberty with the holy. If under God people are the holiest of creations, then it seems logical that to commit the highest form of abuse, idolatry, and worship is to over-prioritize the human body and completely destroy it. Every type of sexual perversion or bodily harm is brought about within a community as a direct result of taking liberties with the holy.

Communities who take liberty with the ultimate Holy—in this instance, with God's Word and God's character—ultimately create worlds that have them at the center. This is where every cult, hierarchical denomination, communistic government, and the like originate. Note, that all the things I mention are based on top-down ideologies. Big personality. Big government. Big headquarters. Making much of _____ (you fill in the blank) Those who consider themselves "big deals" will, at the end of the day, bring scrutiny against even God and his Word. Sadly, having anything in power besides God results in warped views of reality that only works for some people and not others.

What's at stake in all of this? Easy. **Unity.** And hear me now … unity is very different than uniformity. Uniformity sets as its **first** priority what you think and do. To be part of the "club" and whatever that club is, you have to agree with what they think and do. Not only do you have to agree with what they think, but you also have to articulate it, live it out, and imitate it the exact same as the one prescribing the rules. As a result, everyone becomes the same type of person. Uniform. Peer Pressure. Mob. No distinction, no personality, no creativity. Black and white. Vanilla. All disagreement or new ideas are barred and condemned, and everything is silenced except for what comes from the mass voice.

Unity in Diversity, a catchphrase in our culture today, is far different. It's far different than how racial propagandists are using in modern times. Many today use the phrase more in the vein of **Uniform in Diversity**. They are essentially saying, you need to look like us to be diverse. It doesn't make any sense.

Unity …

God's unity begins with **being** and ends in **thinking and doing.** Christ seems to emphasize the type of person we **become** over and above what we **think and do**. We work **from the knowledge that we're God's beloved**, not **for love.** The greatest commandment is to love God and love your neighbor. To love assumes that we are going to do what's best for the other in order to serve them, not ourselves. This assumes we are going to become a certain type of a person, and then our actions will come from that. So what kind of person are you going to look to in order to accomplish *right being*? Before we can start acting (moving forward), we have to know first who we are "being" (after whom are we modeling our existence).

In response to the above, what unites God's body is not a race, creed, gender, science, club, mantra, policy, legislature, contract, or whatever else the world uses to try and create oneness. God's body is united by a physical man. Jesus. The one we look at. The being. The starting place. A perfect image we look to in order to become like him. Gazing upon him causes our life to model **embrace**, **not exclusion.**

Those who operate in uniformity can only hang around people that look like them. Everyone else is excluded. It's the popular crowd mentality. In or out. On the other hand, Jesus is both God and man, and so everyone and everything ultimately comes from him and bears his likeness; even if only in the most faint ways. He's the ultimate end to all inclusion. Embrace. To put it another way, if Jesus were a magnet that was only to vibrate when meeting up with like material, Jesus can literally vibrate and resonate to variant degrees when touching any and all things in the created universe because all things come from him and end in him. What other system or person can say that?

Embrace sees past race, gender, and all the other things and hears the words of Jesus saying "let **all** who are weary and of heavy laden come to me, and let me give them rest" (Mt. 11:28). Jesus' kingdom and all of his creation are literally **from him**, so every personality, male and female, young and old, loud and quiet, sharp and soft, high and low, bright and dull, etc., all have something of his nature to show forth uniquely in brilliance and awe. ***Jesus is the only one that preserves unity in diversity.***

Many might say of Christians that we are bigoted and exclusive, but we are actually the only faith-system in the history of the world, that says "all" can come. We are a model of embrace. Every other community system is based on taking liberty with the holy, divided passions, or creating their own theologies from ideologies. They all have an "in and out line" that followers have to meet to be accepted. Everyone draws the line somewhere and qualifies who can be in or out based on something that is most often times out of a person's control (i.e. race, culture, upbringing, privilege, education level, mental capacity, etc.) Jesus' way is extended to all without condition. He meets the perfect parameters set in order to be accepted, and he simply asks you to accept his work on your behalf.

To bring the argument back to Pastor Warren, Cartwright, and Samson, let's sum it up in Samson's phrase that he spoke when meeting his first wife; "Get her for me, for she is **right in my eyes.**" Samson's world centered around what he deemed right in his eyes. At the moment he labeled this woman in the category of what is good, he condemned God's plan and excluded his parent's questions as they asked: "Is there not a woman among the daughters of your relatives?" In other words, his parents might have said: "Don't you think God, if this is a good situation, would have provided a wife in a way that seems right to him, not you?"

Pastor Warren fits the same bill. Going after sex online seemed right to him, so he took it; never mind the fact that God is painfully clear how sexual satisfaction is achieved—through and in the covenant of marriage between one man and one woman. Warren wanted things that were "right in his own eyes."

It's the **Man Behind the Mask**. The community sees one thing in people who put on masks, but deep under the waves and swells lie motives altogether different. Agendas seem good when they operate for all, but when our own passions are motivating us, they ultimately reveal our true intentions. When we take over, we're only in this for what we get out of it. A community can not benefit from such a situation.

The Remedy? It's three-fold:

1. Hide **In** Theology to Create an Ideology
2. Take Liberty **In** the Holy
3. Maintain Unified Passions

YOU MIGHT BE SAYING to yourself, well, that's the exact list you just got done telling us to avoid. You're correct. When it all comes down to brass tacks, much of what we do in life is not wrong, it's the motivations and objects that we make supreme that often lead us astray.

For example, if I serve a communist leader and I'm in great power, can I create a pretty amazing world for myself? One of great wealth and privilege? Yes! Can I take advantages of the freedoms afforded to me? Yes. Can I go where I please? Yes. Nonetheless, the system I've bought into is abusive and one that leads to bondage for myself and others. So, following the wrong motives, idols, ideologies, and objects, will leave me imperfectly satisfied.

On the contrary, if I turn my affections toward what is most perfect—God the Father, through the Son, in the Power of the Holy Spirit—all the above items in the bulleted list become assets to me. They become inroads to connect people to their deepest desires and to what most deeply satisfies. If Jesus is the source of all goodness, then to drink from his spring is a passionate pursuit of the highest kind.

Let me offer a tidbit that's been helpful for me in thinking about such matters. In science, there's an idea that for every action there's an equal and opposite reaction. A similar reality is true of faith, and yet to a greater degree. For every slavery and bondage, there is *greater freedom.* For every act of sin or unrighteousness, there is a greater way to act in righteousness. To heal from lying, tell the truth. To heal from depression, practice rejoicing. To heal from lust, practice worshipping and "gazing on the beauty of the Lord." To heal from stealing, give. To heal from deception, live vulnerably. To heal from selfishness, serve. To heal from bitterness and hate, waste yourself in loving and apologizing to an enemy. On and on goes the list. Bottom line, we're not victims to our sin. We're culprits. We do the opposite of righteousness when we sin, and we get the logical result. Cause and effect. The powerful truth is that with God, for every evil action, there's a more powerful and opposite action that actually undoes, contradicts, counteracts, and heals all evil.

To break the above ideas down into simpler and practical terms, consider what might be a remedy to Samson and Pastor Warren's lustful eye. A typical Christian response might be to label what Samson and Pastor Warren are doing as wrong. We will tell them to stop, and in an effort to do so we will demonize their passion to pursue sexual desire. In part, we are correct in our advice. In another respect we're not helpful to them in where they are currently because they feel like what they're doing, at least on an instinct level, is right. We must counsel them to avoid the perversion, but to say "don't do that" to someone who wants to means that their flesh will only want to do it more. To live in such a way is to live our lives as Christians on the **defense**. We immediately demonize good things that have just been twisted, and suddenly we turn everything into something to avoid. We place evil behind every bush because everything could lead to sin. Alcohol. Sex. Drugs. Rock n' Roll. Oh my! But being on the defense as a Christian is not helpful. It's actually harmful. It makes our enemy stronger than we are. We are always conscious of how the big dog might jump out and bite us. This is not the mentality of victory.

The truth of the gospel is that Jesus has disarmed the enemy. Satan has no bite. He's not a giant pit bull with strong jaws ready to clamp, he's an ornery little Pekingese who yaps, but cowers when you take one strong step in his direction. Jesus and his power have silenced the beast on land and sea. The victory of Jesus' birth, death, Resurrection, Ascension, and soon to be the Second Coming, are all signs that the Devil's trajectory of strength is growing weaker and weaker and weaker.

In Christ, we hold the upper hand. The life of the Christian is one of **offense**. We do not say "don't do" to anything, but we invite everyone to consider how you can "do all things to the glory of God." For Pastor Warren and Samson, and even Cartwright, this is what they needed to be told. They don't need to hear, "don't have sex, that's bad." They need to embrace the notion; "God has provided a righteous outlet for sexual desire and it's between and man and women in marriage."

Samson ... Pastor Warren ... you need to go home and explore passionate and frequent sex with your wives.

My advice about out-letting sexual desire rightly sounds even more ludicrous than actually encouraging someone to be more sexually active. Sadly, I've had people who are not Christians tell me they can't understand why I would counsel someone to outlet all sexual desire on one person when they "have so many wild oats to sow." My response is to give a statistic. I say to them, "statistics tell us that the average single male has sex one time every thirty days. The average married male in a healthy marriage has sex 3-4 times a week." Doing things God's way actually results in us getting MORE OF OUR DESIRES, not less.

The remedy for Pastor Warren and Samson is to go on offense. They need to be counseled to pursue righteous sex and do it often with their spouse. Cartwright needs to be told to invest as much time into surrender as he does controlling things. It's positively freeing to work hard at the act of letting go. There's a greater reward in pursuing the righteousness of surrender over the unrighteousness of fearful OCD. Actually, the more we release control to something comparatively greater in strength—our God—the more powerful we feel. It's odd how that works. It's a dichotomy.

Bottom line, for every perversion out there, there's a righteous manner in which to go on the offense. We must go on the attack. It preserves the truth. When we go on defense we actually complicate truth. For example, rather than telling someone, "don't drink"—which would exclude many options for an enjoyable and sustainable drink, we must provide people with the wisdom of how to drink righteously. Just saying "don't do" is far too limiting and not biblical. Don't say, don't eat, or don't touch. Those are Paul's words. Rather say, how has God instructed us to eat or touch this or that in a manner that's loving and brings him glory? Don't say, "don't do drugs" because this makes off limits the using of any drugs that are proven to bring health and help to people. We must not be controlled by the perversion of anything, but rather find the righteous and spirit-filled way to enjoy all things that Jesus has filled all in all. To his glory.

This is where the tide changes in regard to **hiding in our theology to create an ideology.** For Samson, Cartwright, and Pastor Warren, they developed a view of God that protected their worldview. Their version of God fit into their box. Their theology became a wall behind which they would hide so that God could only touch or not touch their morality in the places they allowed. They maintained control. Or they created the illusion of control. Living **behind** a wall is different than living **in** a fortress. Walls only protect us when coming from one direction. You can't live behind a wall because you're exposed from three other sides. This is the problem I see with the Warrens, Cartwrights, and Samsons of the world. They will create really safe ways of believing, and yet they will be exposed in a host of other areas. They will ignore other essential things by overcompensating toward other pet peeves.

Take Warren and Cartwright's example, they were hyper-controlling. Why? They had erected theologies that protected their secret or their control. However, they didn't mean every post and the facade of control didn't work. This is how sin rules. It gives a false sense of protection and safety all while keeping someone in the bondage of fear. What forms in us when we live this way is an ideology and vision of the "good life" that is one of self-protection. Love cannot enter nor thrive when self-protection, control, and secrets abound.

God's theology, or the true logic of God, is one of freedom. It's a fortress. Fortresses are different than walls because they surround the believer on every side, and they provide a place for life to flourish within. Now, don't hear me wrong. I'm not saying churches should become fortresses. Most churches are fortresses, and they never venture out, and they stay secluded within their false sense of safety behind four man-made walls. The church is to be an advancing and moving fortress. And let's face it, when in history have you seen one of those?

Constructed human fortress structures are stable and immovable. That's not what I'm talking about here. God's fortress is living and active. God doesn't make us safe with walls, but with principles and paradigms in Scripture that can guide as anywhere and everywhere we go. He says in your sitting, lying down, rising up, or walking along, bind the truths of God to heart. When we carry the truth of God around in this way, we are armed for every good work. We may run into someone's contradictory ideology of the good life at work, school, play, in marketing, architecture, budgets, portfolios, websites, and on and on the list goes, but when we're armed with God's truth we become educated workers in the fields of God's harvest. We see through facades of greed, adultery, deception, manipulation, debt, idol worship, coveting, and all the subtle undercurrents that lie behind the masks of logos, marketing campaigns, business propositions, mission statements and the like, and we hide in our theology. We carry the fortress of God with us.

Carrying God with us allows us to interpret all that comes into our path. We no longer take anything at face value, thus risking getting sucked in and becoming something we are supposed to hate, like in Samson and Pastor Warren's case. We can now thoughtfully think through everything theologically and strip off the paint of perversion and find a way to use and make things in their purest form. Let's face it, because of sin and the long legacy of evil in our world, every good thing often has a thick layer of crap laid on top of it. It takes a while to dig down and find the gold. This is what embracing a thoughtful and sound theology of God does for us. It enables us to interpret everything we encounter in light of God's glory and helps us use everything as a tool to honor him and help others flourish.

We flip the coin in regard to **taking liberty <u>in</u> the holy.** We don't use things for our own selfish desires, but we enjoy things freely in the way God allows. All things are holy for people with holy hearts who use them. God sets proper limits and boundaries on all he creates for our betterment. It's the same way in which a parent loves to watch their children ride bikes in the road, but says ***move when you see cars***. The simple boundary allows the child to experience fun, enjoyment, and expression, all while resting in an assured safety. We need to embrace a common manner of thinking when seeking to find the freedom of Christ in how we use all things. When we use them in the way the Word tells us, we flourish.

The human heart is the foundation of all of the above. Christ says, "It's not what is outside a man that defiles a man, but what comes out of him." If our heart is ugly and perverted, we'll twist everything we touch. If our heart is seeking holiness in Christ and his ways of doing things, then everything we touch, taste, see, feel, and hear becomes a tool with which to honor him.

It is at this moment that our **passions are unified.** Jesus says in Psalms 34:7 that we should "Take delight in the Lord, and he will give you the desires of your heart." This is the sneakiest and cheekiest verse in all of Scripture in my opinion. God's having fun with us. He's saying, I want to give you all your passions, and dreams, and hopes, and desires. The sneaky part is he says, "Take delight in me" before that happens. It's not like setting out as Samson did; in getting what he wanted at the cost of others and his love for God. Samson lived only for his selfish gain but he labeled it as godly.

Delighting in God is altogether different. God sneakily says, look at me—the perfect—until you're satisfied with everything perfect and then go do what you want. What we don't realize in our moments of unity with God is that all the desires we now feel inside and are ready to act on are his. It's a glorious trick. While we seek him, he makes his dreams and aspirations our own, and, therefore, when we go out and pursue our wants wildly, we actually bring him glory. Our passion for our own desires and his desires are now *one*.

A twofold blessing results in a community that starts to heal in these ways. **Wild creativity and flourishing production** become the norm, and an environment of **order, not control** develops. When people begin to realize the right use for things in all of creation, they begin to see the prolific disorder of how the world has commoditized and fashioned everything into objects of use, abuse, consumption, and depletion. The wildness of redeemed creativity develops a vision for innovating. A community that begins to heal regarding leaders like Samson and Pastor Warren and Cartwright are communities that start to see a potential for life beyond our control.

The amazing part about a new redemptive vision is that declining control produces the opposite of chaos. When hearts seek to delight in God first, their creative liberty actually becomes quite helpful and is actually self-protecting. The theology guides the biography. Right believing guards right making. Right thinking leads to right producing.

Herein lies the conundrum for things such as our government of today. Big governments believe that heavier handed and bigger policy structures make for a better world, but it's quite the opposite. God exerts his governing control through the human heart. God's structure is much smaller. It's through the delight of the individual. When this person learns to love, serve, and delight in God, all acts of evil slowly diminish as the heart grows more and more purified, sanctified, and holy underneath the Savior's hand.

Communities that have been led by a tyrant without rails (Samson), a man of secrets behind a mask (Pastor Warren), or a person of manipulation who is overly controlling (Cartwright) tend to exist in a bed of nails. They wonder when and what nail they will step on that will anger the overlord. This strangles exploration and discovery. This kills any chance at creativity and possible failed attempts. This destroys any time that is needed to uncover things that may offer differing opinions, challenge assumptions, or offer real solutions, instead of always talking about the problems.

We heal not by just saying, "Jesus saves sinners," although this is true, one must ask, "what does that look like?" One that is saved acts different and is different, and makes different choices. In a place where misdirected passions rule, an offender and the offended must be given a different road on which to run fast. In lives where control or a misuse of holy things reigns, a person can only heal when they are allowed to taste the freedom that surrender brings and the joy found in being taught how to use things rightly.

QUESTIONS FOR DISCUSSION

First, contemplate these questions individually and answer in the space provided, and then join together collectively as a group. Here are some Scriptures that can help guide your discussion:

Verses to Consider: *The Story of Samson in Judges 13-16*

1. Have we as communities contributed to the growing statistics of fallen leaders in our midst in the church?

2. What are ways in which we actually allow for secrecy and shame to go unnoticed in the community of God, rather than putting in place things that invite safety through confession and openness?

. . .

3. In what ways is the telling of Samson's story in this book different from how you've heard it shared previously?

4. Are we seeing a "case of the Samsons" in our culture today? Meaning, are we seeing that many have a disconnect between what they say they believe and how they actually act?

5. How do we make deeper and intentional connections between our actions and beliefs?

6. What desires or divided passions do you struggle with?

7. What are the righteous ways in which to fulfill your wrongly expressed desires, and how can you pursue the righteous ways of meeting your needs today?

8. Describe what it means to *take liberty with the holy*?

9. Upon reading this book, how much did you value your theology's connection to every matter of your life? After reading, can you see how everything we do comes down to our actions based on a theology—a belief in whatever we prize as ultimate?

10. How can you actively grow in your diet and learning of theology in order to work on your view of God and better your service unto him?

2 / CLOSING THOUGHTS

... I thank him who has given me strength, Christ Jesus our Lord, because he judged me faithful, appointing me to his service, though formerly I was a blasphemer, persecutor, and insolent opponent. But I received mercy because I had acted ignorantly in unbelief, and the grace of our Lord overflowed for me with the faith and love that are in Christ Jesus. The saying is trustworthy and deserving of full acceptance, that Christ Jesus came into the world to save sinners, of whom I am the foremost. ***But I received mercy for this reason, that in me, as the foremost, Jesus Christ might display his perfect patience as an example to those who were to believe in him for eternal life****. To the King of the ages, immortal, invisible, the only God, be honor and glory forever and ever. Amen.*

- 1 Timothy 1:12-17

In closing this book, I'd like to leave you with the above Scripture to ponder and consider. We've considered the idea of *Following the Fallen*, and this is by no means a new concept in the church or in our fallen world. You are fallen. Those whom you love, work under, work for, serve around, and play beside, are all going to fall pleasantly into one category—fallen. Logically, it is correct for us to assume that any and every situation we walk into will be fraught with problems. By the off chance you walk into a perfect scenario, you will find that it will quickly be thrown into chaos because you're there.

Let's face the truth, we bring imperfect with us.

The Scripture above from 1 Timothy can help us to embrace our mistakes and all our sinfulness with a lot of encouragement and glory. Consider Paul, the speaker of this passage. Paul gives his rap sheet, his resume, and his credentials. They are not very positive. As you can see, Paul has a lot to learn about selling himself in order to get a great job that pays well. As Paul prattles on about his days as a persecutor of the church and a murderer of Christians, note how he recounts the events of his salvation, and the reasons he gives for that salvation. He concludes that in all his horrible fallen ugliness, God's plan all along was to ***display his (Jesus) perfect patience in him (Paul) as an example to those who were to believe in him (Jesus) for eternal life.***

We might need some courage to arrive at the same conclusions as Paul when it comes to our situation: considering those that have hurt us or in regard to the sins we've committed that have harmed others. I mean, it's ludicrous, right? To conclude that the Almighty God of the universe might want to ***put on display*** something of his beauty via our most hideous sin? It's crazy. Yet, it makes sense.

Think for a moment about the fruit of the spirit: love, joy, peace, patience, kindness, goodness, gentleness, faithfulness, and self-control. All of these attributes of God can not be seen in their full beauty without an opposing adversary. It is easy to love a lovable friend, but where the true depth of love is tested is when love reaches to save the most vengeful enemy. Gentleness shows its greatest power when it is the softest while under attack. Patience is made glorious when there is much to be patient about, and the same is true of all the other fruit listed.

In Luke 14:13-14, Jesus echoes the above sentiment when he says, "but when you give a feast, invite the poor, the crippled, the lame, the blind, and you will be blessed because they cannot repay you. For you will be repaid at the resurrection of the just." Jesus reveals here that true generosity—the kind that heaven and the kingdom of God are known for—is found when someone gives without limit and without any hope of being repaid. In essence, the truest and most beautiful test of the giver is to give to one who is unable to repay or one who will repay the given kindness with nothing but a whining and ungrateful heart.

God is trying to put his beauty on display in the horrors of your situation. Plain and simple. You may be serving under a class-A controller. You may be that person. You may currently be under the spell of a manipulator, or you may struggle with it yourself. You may know the false teacher, follow the bells and whistles, or you may even be a recovering sex offender or adulterer. Whatever your shame, and whatever your baggage, I can't help but lump you into Paul's statement. I can't help but assume that if God can be glorified through a "Murderer of Christians," that God might have something specific to put on display in you or your situation today.

I want to leave you with the sentiment and thought that God is putting something about himself on stage in your current pain. Chances are, you're following someone and their falseness is, has, or will really impact and affect you. You will in turn affect them. Many of you are already identifying with many of the scenarios

I've offered in this book, and you may be thinking "that's me" or "that's him," but I'd venture to guess that it hasn't even dawned on you to think about how God's glory might be on display in the fallenness you're encountering. That's the fault of our current condition as humans. When someone falls, commits a sin, abuses someone, abuses power, conceals, breaks trust, and the like, we instantly take the defensive and see nothing but bad in the situation. Have you followed modern-day news reporting? Emphasizing the bad is what sells. God, on the other hand, when the horror occurs, thinks, "Now how can I use this to show all involved the depths of my healing and my perfect glory?" Jesus uses our broken moments to drive us to himself. It's for our good and for his glory.

So, might I ask you who are dealing with a fallen person caught in sin today to ask "What is God trying to display in this situation?" Rather than trying to fix the offender and becoming just as guilty as they are yourself, stop and pray. Ask the merciful God of heaven to teach you how he restores the darkest of hearts. Ask the God of grace how he can mend the most damaged, secretive, deceptive, and destructive of lives, and how he can bring greater things about through tragedy than we might possibly venture to fathom.

Hear what I'm saying. I'm not saying that we become determinists and see God as the boogeyman behind every bush of evil and of good, but we must realize that God is most certainly present, active, aware, and maneuvering everything for good in EVERY situation. Concluding that God's presence is with us even amidst the most surprising and awful events and occurrences is the greatest Shalom that we have.

Take this book. Take it to heart. Don't wield it like a sword at others who have hurt you. Don't ignore the surgery that this book can do upon your soul. Let this book soak into you and make you a more gracious, loving, wise, and forgiving person. Let's face it, there are too many people out there throwing stones. We need more people around that are equipped to pick up and heal the broken pieces. That's what this book is about. Equipping. To build you up. To heal.

It is my prayer that to some degree this book has helped you feel trained. My prayer is that God would continue to equip you as you seek his redemptive purposes through all those fallen.

www.ingramcontent.com/pod-product-compliance
Lightning Source LLC
Chambersburg PA
CBHW070137100426
42743CB00013B/2737